T0272106

A Stroke of
HOPE

Surviving a Hemorrhagic Stroke

LESLIE DORR DERRIG

authorHOUSE®

AuthorHouse™
1663 Liberty Drive
Bloomington, IN 47403
www.authorhouse.com
Phone: 833-262-8899

Published by AuthorHouse 06/19/2024

ISBN: 979-8-8230-2821-9 (sc)
ISBN: 979-8-8230-2822-6 (e)

Library of Congress Control Number: 2024911606

Print information available on the last page.

Any people depicted in stock imagery provided by Getty Images are models, and such images are being used for illustrative purposes only. Certain stock imagery © Getty Images.

This book is printed on acid-free paper.

Introduction

It has been a little over 3 years since my 75-year-old husband had a hemorrhagic stroke (brain bleed) of the Thalamus part of his brain. I have wanted to keep a blog going all this time, but never had the time or the drive to write it all down and remember everything. Life has gotten easier and improved to the point where I cannot wait to share his story.

This is my story about my husband, the patient, and me, the caretaker. When my husband had an inner brain bleed or better known as a hemorrhagic stroke of the Thalamus, I could not find much online to explain what I was going to experience. The blogs were so short, it was like the bloggers had given up. At the hospital and at rehab, no one really gave us hope and direction; I felt lost and hopeless.

I only ask that when you read this, you recognize I am not a writer, a medical professional, or rolling in the dough. We are not on Medicaid where everything is paid for; we did this recovery on a shoestring budget, with love and a lot of prayer. It is not my intention to bring on the tears but to bring out the joy knowing there is hope when everyone else says, "Sorry, this is how it is going to be for the rest of your life.

Nov. 10, 2017, 6:30 AM I rolled over in bed and saw that my husband, Bill, was up; he never gets up that early.... NEVER! I found him on the toilet upstairs where he had been pushing with no results, but his comments were, "I do not feel right, I'm a little woozy." I had suggested he had possibly been on the toilet too long and that he should get up and walk around and lay back down. When he got up, he was off balance and dizzy and grabbing for the kitchen counter to hold himself up. He then decided he wanted to go back downstairs to bed. I got in front of him, doing my best to hold him up, he then grabbed the top of the banister at the top of the stairs and collapsed on top of me. My heart was in my throat as I envisioned the two of us tumbling together down the long wooden stairs. With my heart rushing and adrenaline at its peak, I pushed my 250 lb., 6'5" husband backward and onto the floor. He was deadweight, but I never ever had such a rush of strength as I did then. I knew immediately it was a stroke.

I quickly pushed him more and dragged his lifeless body away from the top of the stairs so that I could get by him and get to my phone. All of a sudden, my brain kicked into motion, and I controlled my hysteria. I remember my words exactly:

911: "911, what is your emergency? Fire, Police, or Medical?"
Me: "Medical"
New 911 operator: "What is your emergency?"

Me: "My husband had a stroke; he has passed out and is unresponsive. He is 6'5", 250 lbs. and the help has to climb 3 stories in order to get to him, bring extra help. He has a defibrillator and a pacemaker; they have not gone off."

911: "We are sending the ambulance right away with extra help, stay calm."

Within minutes the ER/Firefighters were at my door, all 6 of them. I had taken the time to drag him away from the front door so I could let the crew in. It all happened so fast, it was hard to remember all the intricacies of what happened, but all I heard was, "Yes mam, he has had a stroke" and off they went with him on the gurney and sirens blaring.

The Warwick Firefighters had come prepared, all 6 of them. They carried him down two flights on the chair gurney and were in constant communication with the trauma staff at the hospital; they had prepared the hospital staff with all the vitals so that when he arrived, they could easily take over and start his care.

It was amazing and so surreal; I never thought in a million years I would be so calm and together. Somehow, I had conveyed all of his information, retrieved all of his emergency cards, told them where I wanted him to go, and did not get hysterical. Not one tear, no shakes, and no screaming; I was level-headed.

I got dressed in yesterdays clothes, grabbed my computer, my phone, and my purse, and was out the door in 5 minutes. I made it to the hospital in record time and only ran one inconvenient stop light. Fortunately, Bill had a handicapped placard in the window, so when I pulled up to the hospital valet automatically took my car. I ran to the ER window, and they immediately led me to the trauma room that was set up specifically for strokes.

I walked into the hospital trauma room and there he was, only ½ hour since he had the stroke, laying on a gurney, awake and talking, cracking jokes, and hooked up to all kinds of tubes. You could see the seriousness in everyone's face, they were working with little time, and they did not have much to work with. The ER doctor who specialized in strokes pulled me aside to explain what they were doing and the seriousness of his stroke. The doctor's first question was, "How much do you know about the brain?" I had explained how I have had a minigenome (a non-malignant tumor) removed from my Occipital and my Medulla tapped and drained, so I know a little bit. She then said, "Well Bill's case is a lot more dangerous, have you ever heard of the Thalamus?"

She went on to explain in a calm way, "The Thalamus is located in the center of your brain and looks like a walnut; He had a brain hemorrhage in that area." They then took me to the CT scan which showed the bleed, explaining that if the bleed did not stop it would go to the left side of the Thalamus, and then he would lose his speech, so it was very important that I keep talking to him and have him talk to me. As it was now, he was "only" paralyzed on his left side.

Have you ever felt like your heart stop and your stomach just dropped to the point where you needed to go poop? OMG! All I could say was "DO NOT LOSE IT! LISTEN TO WHAT THEY ARE TELLING YOU AND TAKE IT ALL IN, IT IS NOT ABOUT ME!"

The nurses and the team of doctors went on to talk to me with Bill by my side, and took me over to the computer to show me the bleeding in his brain and explain the details of their concerns and what they were working with; all the while I am talking with Bill and trying to be light-hearted, letting him know he is going to be ok.

The experts first explained the difference between a brain bleed stroke, a blood clot, an aortic stroke, and a hemorrhagic stroke; noting that all of your friends are going to come to you as experts because their relative or friend went through this, and they are back to normal. They went on to tell me all strokes are different and there is so much to learn about strokes that it is hard to explain to everyone.

The brain is protected with many layers so that if you fall and crack your skull, blood will not touch the brain. However, in the event you have a bleed inside the brain, the iron in the blood kills the brain cells and that part does not recover. It is important to stop the bleeding ASAP, so no further damage is done to the brain itself.

I thought I knew everything about the brain as I have a meningioma that constantly needs attention, so I studied the brain like it was the computer of my body. However, I had never even heard of the Thalamus.

It is the size of a walnut, and it is in two sections: the left and the right. The right side of the Thalamus controls the left side of your body's functions, and the left side controls the speech and right side of your body. Bill's was on his right side and he became paralyzed right down the middle of his body from the top of his head to the toes. For this reason, the trauma nurse kept on having me talk to him to make sure he did not slur his words. As he started to slow his words, she pulled me aside.

This is something that I have repeated over and over again to everyone: "Do you know all of your husband's passwords and IDs to his computer and phone?" "WHAT? IDs and passwords?" Of course, I know them; WRONG! The nurse could see where this was going and quickly gave me a Sharpie, I grabbed a paper towel, and from there, Bill released all of the keys to everything. If I had waited one more minute or if the bleed had gone to the other side, things would have been a lot more complicated than they already were.

Just as I got the ID and PW I was rushed out of the room; another stroke patient had just come in and I needed to make room and give them privacy. The ER Trauma doctor pulled me into another room where he showed me the bleed again on his screen and explained how dangerous this type of stroke was. He gave me so much information that I felt comfortable and in control of my emotions because I knew exactly what we were dealing with. The doctor also explained that normally he would order an MRI, but because of his defibrillator and pacemaker, they could only do a CT scan, and that they were going to have to do it again to make sure the bleed had stopped.

At this point I could still not go in to see Bill, they were working on his roommate, and they needed the room. Sadness filled the room; the new stroke patient had passed. This poor young man had been going through so much chemo that it had weakened him. He had a DNR, and they respected his wishes.

I then called our daughters and friends to let them know what we were dealing with. It was my first update since I had called from the car on the way to the hospital. I had silenced my phone so it would not go off in the room, and I had missed so many of the calls requesting updates. Our daughter in California had silenced her phone, so when she woke up to her voicemail and read my text at 5:00 AM PDT, we were already in the thick of discovery and too much information was coming our way.

As I was talking to our daughters, they moved out the young man who had passed and immediately brought in a young girl who was suffering a stroke. They immediately moved her up to the OR and cleaned up the room. While I had stepped out to make phone calls, they had taken Bill in to get another CT scan. When I arrived back to the room, his gurney was gone, and he was too! I almost lost it again; they saw my white face and quickly assured me he would be right back; they were just doing another CT. Phew! That was a heartstopper.

They let me know that it appeared that his bleeding had stopped and now they were trying to determine the depth of the damage to his brain and how much paralysis he would have. It was only 9:30 AM and in 3-short hours I had gone from a normal happy life to dealing with the uncertainty of my husband's life. This was a whole new world, and the realization was mind-boggling. I wanted to stop the world and try and catch up to the spinning. I started praying like I had never prayed before. I needed intervention!

Two young ladies came down from the research department and asked permission to talk to me regarding a clinical trial they could offer to Bill. I am a huge fan of clinical trials, so I was all ears. They had explained how time was of the essence and we needed to work on this right away. They interviewed me for about half an hour to determine if he was the perfect candidate and eligible for this trial. It was the 2nd stage of a long trial and there was only 1 slot left out of the 500. After the long questionnaire, they determined he was a perfect candidate, beating out the other guy who was in Indianapolis hoping he would be the recipient. There was no guarantee he would not get the placebo and that the results of the trial would change him, but I was willing to go to bat for my husband.

The idea of the clinical trial was to do 3-bag drips into the bloodstream over a period of 3 days. They commented that their trial was to remove the iron in the bloodstream, as it was the iron in the blood that kills the brain and the brain cells. It was a surprise to me that the brain is never in contact with blood; the veins and arteries go through the brain, but it never is in direct contact. Once the brain is in contact with the blood, it is the iron that destroys the brain. Needless to say, it was a "No-Brainer" to say yes, let's give him the trial.

The research department gave me so much information and calmness that I really felt empowered; it gave us real hope. I went back into the Trauma Room to talk more with Bill, who had dosed off out of boredom, so I talked more with the team. They told me they would be moving him up to the ICU on the Stroke Floor and they were just preparing his room. Then I was pushed out of the room again, another stroke victim! It was only 11:00 now. I mentioned to the doctor that I was surprised that there were so many stroke victims that morning. He then explained to me that there are so many different kinds of strokes, but that this morning the moon was aligned, and they were dealing with a lot more than usual. He explained they were dealing with mostly blood-clot strokes and not actual brain hemorrhages like Bill was going through. He let me know that with a hemorrhagic stroke if you are on blood thinners, had taken a baby aspirin, or had orange juice that morning we would not be talking like we were. He said this is why very few survive Thalamus strokes.

I, the layman, became a sponge and soaked up as much information as I could and asked questions of the trained minds and superior doctors who had dedicated their lives to this field of expertise. I swear to this day, it was the listening and asking questions and totally understanding every little detail that put me to rest. I felt empowered and transferred all of that onto Bill and our daughters.

With Clinical Trials, you never know if you are getting the real drug or placebo. You go on living your life hoping you were the lucky one. I knew one way or the other it was not going to hurt him, but I had hoped it would help him. Since the Clinical Trial had been in its 3rd stage, they had already made it through the other 2 stages without a problem. He was the last dose they had left so the trial was coming to an end. One and a half years later, I found out he got the placebo, and the trial never passed to an authorized form of treatment.

Daughters

I am not a weak woman; I am strong and feel I can get through anything. I know my friends and family all look at me as if I were superwoman because I have handled all of Bill's near-death experiences, surgeries, and emergencies, and still manage to work full-time, keep a big house that always needs work, clean and make dinner, and run two large community events each year. Yes, I do all of that, but it is because I like to do it, it is fulfilling, and I really like to stay busy. I am very religious and believe that God helps those who help themselves and helps others.

However, if you think I am a superwoman, you have not met my daughters. If there was ever a super proud mama out there, it is me. I am always enamored by how much they do with their careers, children, and lives; Bill and I are soooo blessed to have two remarkable daughters.

I say all of that because I can say without thought, that if it were not for my daughters, we would not have gained as much information as we did to help Bill. Once they had all of the diagnoses and intricate details of his new body, they went to town in the research department.

Danielle, who at that time, had an almost 2-year-old and a 14-year-old. She is a principal at a new dual language elementary school in the lower Bronx, married, and a soccer mom. She juggled her life like I never could and still managed to drive 4-hours every Friday after school and leave late on Sunday nights to get back to work. Every day, she would call in 3 to 4 times a day with a new idea she had researched and call in with ideas she had found.

Gabrielle is a full-time personal trainer, a mother of then a 5- and 6-year-old boy and girl and has a husband who travels. With her background as a doctor of Chinese Medicine, she tapped her friends to see what ideas they had and if they would be willing to help out.

My dear friend and acupuncturist, Dr. Mark, said he would definitely come and work on him. However, the hospital would not allow him to come in and give him acupuncture, so we got him to work behind closed curtains. We snuck him in on a Sunday and he was able to get good responses, but once the hospital staff got wind of what we were doing, they stopped his treatment. We snuck him in again and were more careful, but it was obvious they were watching us like a hawk.

One of the online searches Danielle came up with was a company called Flint Rehab. It had everything! It clarified everything for us in print and gave us a wealth of knowledge. Danielle would come up on the weekends and do various treatments and tests on his body that she would have read about. Gabrielle would do other searches on various treatments and then we'd share them with the therapists.

They both worked so hard behind the scenes; I was heartfelt by their support. I was so proud of the strong women that we had raised and could not keep my emotions in check every time they came through for us. Family means everything when you go through this kind of event. More on this later.

Friends

One of the first things I did was to call some very close friends of ours. I knew they would want to know, the two of them do so much with us as friends. They also got into the research and discovery of various treatments and the need to stay positive. They came to see him almost every weekend, all the way from Connecticut; it was their commitment to our friendship and closeness that kept them nearby. The husbands are the same age, and the two wives are too; we vacation together, and they own a summer house near us. They are like our brother and sister.

I knew many people wanted to come and see Bill, but I encouraged them to bring their "A-Game" and keep it light with hope. Everyone knows I am light-hearted, do not take myself too seriously, and want everyone else to laugh too. Our friends, John & Nancy, decided to do a "Joke-a-Day" and would call in the morning to give Bill a good laugh. Bill in turn searched the staff to get him a joke to share too, so he could also make them laugh. Like they say, "Laughter is the best medicine." He would share these jokes with the staff, and they were actually looking forward to coming into the room to laugh and get the next joke.

We belong to a very strong community church with a very

committed fellowship. It is not a bible-beating, hell-be-damned church, it is a church of wonderful people who are all out to help each other and support whoever is in need, all while enjoying life. Everyone is friends and everyone is there to be there for you. When I tell you, everyone came out of the woodwork to help us, sent cards, and offered assistance. There was so much compassion that it was humbling.

Bill and I had cleaned up our diets for the past year and we were focusing on everything organic; lots of organic greens, grass-fed, no antibiotics, no fried, no gluten, no yeast, minimal sugar, and no preservatives…. In other words, very restrictive. He was worse about this than I was, but I went along with it and cheated when he was out of site. Bill was so committed to this new way of eating that I knew I had to keep it up for him; I brought him all his meals to the hospital; yes, every meal. However, so many people wanted to bring us (me) meals, and I knew I could not eat them. I knew Bill would have a canary if he found out I was cheating, so I tried hard to let people know I appreciated their kindness, but he would not allow us off the restrictions. If you know our church, you know you will never be hungry if someone is sick in your house and you need meals; they are the most generous people.

So, what do you bring someone like that? He would eat nuts (not peanuts), dark chocolate, hummus, cheese, packaged salads from Trader Joe's, organic vegetable trays, packaged sushi, fish, chicken, eggs, and his Bulletproof Coffee. I know several people had comments of despair, but I knew I could not go against him at this time of his recovery. Then people asked if they could bring him a book or magazines; what could I say, he could not focus, and reading was just not going to happen for quite a while. He tried the Audible books but would fall asleep in 3 minutes flat.

The issue was more that he could not focus his eyes and listening to Podcasts or books made him fall asleep. So many people wanted to come and visit, and I knew it was what he needed most. But he would either fall asleep or be in another world when they would come. I had to work around his therapy schedule. He would sleep before therapy, come back from therapy, and then sleep some more. I would ask people to call me in advance so I could schedule their visit, but I could tell, his schedule did not always match his friends. It was difficult, but we managed. I just wanted to make sure he stayed on his schedule and was strong enough for his therapy. They had told me that sleep was the best thing for a stroke patient.

Friends are the best, especially when you are afflicted with a debilitating event like a stroke or paralysis. I knew if I was depressed, he had to be even more depressed. I knew coming to see him twice a day was extremely important, and it would give him something to look forward to, but cards were the best thing since sliced bread. It was his food for the brain, it was great for his depression, and it made him feel like no one had forgotten him.

I had started emailing a chain of friends from the beginning, keeping them updated like a blog. It was the best thing for me, I could not work and take phone calls or write emails all day long and still be good for Bill. I knew everyone had the kindest hearts and their concerns were real. I asked everyone to flood him with cards of hope and the funnier the better. I asked to have kids draw pictures and keep everything happy.

In the beginning, I would tape them to his windows and walls and make sure he could see them all. After the hospital staff complained, I took yards of thin ribbon, tied larger paperclips, and strung the ribbon all around the room. There were literally hundreds of cards and very few repeats. He would look at these cards on the wall and say, "No one has forgotten about me, look how many people care." You could see, it made him feel like a loved man and that he had the support of people he didn't even know. Staff would come by his room and remark on all the cards and how loved he was and what a wonderful idea to put them on a ribbon. I went back and forth on his window, pinning the ribbon to the drapes. It was a great window cover.

When his friends would come, they kept it fun, told jokes, made light of his stroke, and brought dark chocolate and nuts. Did I tell you? I like dark chocolate and nuts too.

A New in Our Book

I slowly learned this was going to be a new life for both of us. It was like a new chapter in our book, but it was more than that, it was not how we had planned it to be. We had spent the last 20 years working on our beach house and making it perfect for our retirement. We had put so much sweat and money into the house, it was our baby. Now everyone was telling me that Bill's stroke was going to change everything. In essence, what they were saying was that your Go-Go years are done, you are on to your No-Go years before you even retire.

Yes, I knew it was going to change everything, but did the medical staff have to be so callous about it? I had just spent the last 20 years with my husband building the house we loved to live in, he had retired, and we were ready to enjoy life.

Weekly, the staff would ask to have a meeting with me to help me prepare for my new life. Every week they wanted me to totally understand the system, how Medicare works, and what insurance did not cover. However, the worst part was when they were trying to get me to understand that after the rehab at the hospital, he would go into a nursing home for rehab and from there he would go home. They had strongly suggested I sell my house and start looking for either an assisted living facility or a nursing home. The timeline I had to work with was so short I knew I could not possibly work with this schedule; it was way too much to take in.

Cry? Cry? I cried so much that I would run out of tears. From the time he had his stroke, I would contain myself as much as possible, and then as soon as I walked to my car at the hospital, I would let it flow. I needed windshield wipers for my eyes so I could see driving home at night. I would talk on the phone from the time I left for the hospital 'til I went to bed. I have to confess, I did eat garbage food and I did drink a couple of shots of Scotch before I went to bed, everything we had sworn off was now on my pallet. I would get myself to sleep and then wake up hysterical; I was not getting good sleep at all and I had stopped working out. I was a basket-case, and I knew many people saw it and were reluctant to say anything. Everyone knew from my emails that I was not on strong footing.

I would go to church and break down. I sat in the back so no one could watch me lose it. I was red-eyed and swollen from my constant crying. People would try to comfort me, but it only made me worse. I would not even listen to the service or songs; I would just pray the entire time. I prayed for everything under the sun and begged for help from God. I'd pray to God for the strength to keep going and stay positive for Bill. I would pray for God to give Bill the strength to hold it together and keep going and get his strength to walk again. There were so many prayer groups set up for him all around the country and so many would send me notes of how their prayer group met and prayed for Bill, and how they could feel the power bestowed on Bill. It meant so much to me that so many people were thinking of him.

I knew we were in for a long battle and recovery, and I knew there would be so many hurdles to get through that I had to constantly think things over, write them down, and research them. This new chapter in my life was not going to be my best chapter, but it was not going to be my last. I knew if we were going to keep our "book of life" interesting, I was going to have to grab the bull by the horns and not let go. I knew it was not going to be easy and I could not give up; he was depending on me, and I had to remember to take care of myself too.

Bill's Near-Death Life

I know that sounds redundant, near-death and near life, but it is so true with him. For over 10 years prior to his stroke, he had lived on the cusp of death, and fortunately, I was with him when it happened. Each time, he has been shocked back to life, recovered, and lived another day.

His first real bad occurrence was when he breathed in airborne Rhino dung dust at the San Diego Adventure Park. Yes, I did say inhaled Rhino dung dust. That bacteria bore 3 holes in his duodenal and he bled out. He had less than 40% of his blood left in his body. As much as I could write a full chapter on this, I will limit my comments to: He died, he came back, he died, he came back, they just kept on shocking him and infusing him until his heart would stop attacking for about 6 hours. The stars were aligned, and we had all the right things happening for him that night. The EMTs diagnosed him right away, Columbia Presbyterian Hospital was right around the corner, the doctor (who was Bill Clinton's Cardiologist) was there, and the ER doctor specialized as a wartime medic on the battlefield and all of them knew what to do. It was touch and go for 3 weeks, but he pulled through. After 21 days in the Cardiac ICU at Columbia Presbyterian, he had a pacemaker implanted; evidently, the lack of blood to his heart damaged his heart muscles and it would just stop beating. Later, he had a defibrillator installed internally that also paced his heart.

After several occurrences of having small heart "pains", he then had the "big" one; a ventricular cardio infarction, commonly known as V-Fib, where the bottom part of your heart beats out of control. As Bill would put it, "I had "Events!", not Heart Attacks." He would fall to the ground and not have a heartbeat, but "OK, so if you had not been zapped back, your heart would have blown up and you would be dead." To me that is not an event, that is an attack. When you are with no pulse and 6-guys lift you to a gurney and run with your 6'5" 250 lb. body hanging over all sides of the bed, totally limp and shove you into the ambulance and start shocking you, I would say you are dead. All of the neighbors were there to watch, including my grandson and his buddies. One neighbor took me in his car right behind the ambulance as the boys went over to his house. Needless to say, no one knew for hours if he made it and horror fell over the neighborhood. They were relieved to know he made it and that he was transferred to a Cardiac Trauma unit.

Once, I drove him to the hospital because he did not want an ambulance, letting them know I was bringing him in. The ER would then shock him. His heart would either stop altogether and they would bring him back, or they would electively shock him to shock the heart to a normal rhythm from 250-300 BPM to 60 BPM. A couple of times they shocked him in the ambulance to bring him back, but I was to understand that this was an "Event" not an attack.

After four major V-Tacks, he had a defibrillator implanted; it was designed to shock the heart muscles to a normal rhythm, and, if your heart did not respond, it would give you a donkey kick to the other side of the room and hope your heart would beat normally. That never happened and his defibrillator did work several times, and his pacemaker did kick in, but the apparatus worked like it was supposed to.

Bill had so much pain in his right knee and left hip, that what he should have done years before was now imperative to be done immediately. He insisted he was in great shape and could handle any pain and he could have both done at the same time. With his insistence, the doctor agreed to do them at the same time because Bill wanted to get back to work. I do not think the nice orthopedic doctor will ever look at someone who was so convincing again and give in to their wishes. To make another long story short, his recovery went from worse to worser and he hobbled around right up to the stroke. He did have to have his hip done again a year later as the long post that goes into the femur needed to be longer.

Then, one day he ran a really high fever of 104 and it would not break. I drove him to the ER and took my number in the queue with everyone who was using the ER as a clinic for splinters and colds. I had demanded a wheelchair when I took him to the door, saying he was a heart patient, and his fever was 104. They checked him out and said he was at no risk of a heart attack and had us sit in the ER with the others to wait our turn. I will not get into my anger and personal feelings about what had transpired for 4 hours, but after I had had it, I went back to the staff in charge of bringing in the patients by number and said, "I am going to call my very close friend ("Mr. So & So" on the hospital board) and let them know how we are being treated here! Look at my husband, his fever is off the charts, and he is delirious, he needs attention now." As I faked my call to someone I did not even know, they took us in. The doctors saw him and started moving so fast you would have thought they were playing beat-the-clock. They thought for sure he had Meningitis, but it only ended up as a Staph infection of the inside of his heart. ONLY!

After a week in ICU and Cardiac care, surgery to remove the defibrillator and pacemaker, and massive doses to rid the Staph inside the heart, he came home with an external vest he had to wear full-time with an external defibrillator and pacemaker. With twice daily nursing staff at home to change bandages and check on him, he was on the mend and spent 3 months in the hot summer with the vest. Three months later, he got a new defibrillator/pacemaker implant.

Bill still had episodes, so the doctor suggested he have an ablation for his ventricular tachycardia. The specialist did a great job in going to the outside of his heart and cauterizing the areas of his ventricles where he was fibrillating. About a year later, they determined that the muscles on the inside of his heart were also in need of an ablation (cauterizing), but his situation required a specialist who was at Boston General. Trying to get into the "only doctor in New England" who does this surgery takes a long wait, and then we found out this doctor was leaving and moving to Virginia. I guess Bill was the last surgery this doctor performed, and it was a success. He later had the defibrillator/pacemaker reinstalled and stayed for a week in the hospital while they fine-tuned it and the drugs, he needed to not reject it. Yay! I could finally take my foot off the gas and rest.

Through all of this, I was working full-time and traveling every other week, and Bill was trying to work as a full-time Project Manager. Eight months before the stroke, he had fully retired at the age of 72.

The First Week
of his Stroke

After the initial shock and awe of the stroke, we all seemed to have accepted our new life. We were all willing to do whatever we could to accept what was real and do what we could to make it so Bill understood we were with him and not giving up. It was obvious to him that we cared, but what we had to make known was, "we were in control."

I had so many people in the hospital who had given me such bleak hope and despair by having me look at the negative side of his recovery. I am not a negative person and I do not do well with negativity; in fact, I will come back at you with rage when you talk of defeat. I guess I did that too much, as I know when they got my phone calls, they ignored them. I know they are told to say certain things and they feel they have to have you face reality, but what is reality? Reality is what you make of it and accept. My reality was, show me how can I find a way to get him to walk? How can I get him to be functional? He cannot have a life of lying in a bed or sitting in a chair.

One of the hospital neurologists saw my strength and determination to make Bill whole again and give him strength. He carefully approached me with one of the best books written about hemorrhagic strokes and suggested I read it slowly and know there is hope. He gave me so much optimism just with his words and confidence that there was hope. This book, "The Brain that Changes Itself," written by Norman Doidge, M.D., was all about how you could train your brain to change how it functions. Usually, the left side of the brain controls the right side and right side controls the left. This book highlighted many true stories how others have dealt with brain injuries and trained the other side of the brain to do the work.

Repetition and perseverance, not letting the struggles stop you from pushing harder; those are the lessons of this book and being confident with your dreams for recovery. As time went by, Bill looked at his thumb, telling it to move, and it would not budge. Then he put the other working thumb next to it and told it to move. Miracle of miracles, on the 5th try it moved. The same thing with the big toe, but that took a little longer; it was a twitch on the 10th try and a move on the 20th attempt. Bingo! That big toe looked so big in all our eyes. He kept practicing this and started mastering "Train Your Brain."

Totally Bombarded

I remember everything hitting me that first week. I was so overloaded with paperwork, insurance issues, and taking care of my home front. I brought my computer with me all the time, I kept a file where I stowed all the paperwork, and I wrote down everyone's name that came into the room and took down phone numbers and job titles. My files were so extensive, but it paid off. It was obvious to everyone; I was in charge, and I was not going to take "no" for an answer. Bill kept his mouth shut and would just say, "Talk to my wife."

I literally set up my office in his hospital room; I had so much to do and keep up with, it was so consuming, and I knew I could not stop working. My office knew what happened to Bill and was very compassionate, but I did not share it with my clients. I remember previously commenting about Bill's hospitalization & heart issues to two separate executives and they went on like I was to keep working at the same pace and not disrupt their requests. They would never ask how he was doing. That's business. I love working and I was not about to quit. I eventually shared with them what I had been going through when I was in a face-to-face meeting with them, but I did not ask for empathy.

Days later, after he was stabilized in the ICU, they moved Bill up to the rehab floor. They said that once they feel patients are medically safe from any more bleeds, they like to get them into therapy right away. Two times a day they did physical therapy for one hour and then occupational therapy once a day for 45 minutes. Bill kept on falling asleep due to the high doses of drugs they were giving him for spasms. They would give him his rehab schedule the day before, so he would then set his phone alarm to wake up in time, but he would fall asleep during his treatment. Spasms after a right brain hemorrhage stroke are prevalent in the paralyzed leg. How they treat these spasms is so difficult, and the pain is screaming pain that cannot be controlled. Bill never gets carried away with pain, but he was yelling daily for months with the pain. They tried so many drugs on him that he could not stay awake.

Dr. James Castle of North Shore University wrote: "With regard to the limb pain, this is very common after a thalamic stroke. It is similar to the phantom limb pain people complain about after a limb amputation - the body simply doesn't know how to interpret a lesion in the sensory neurons coming from the limb through the thalamus, and mis-interprets this as pain." But no one seemed to know this. Dr. Castle even goes on to list the medicines he would recommend for treatment. Now, if I can find this, why can't the doctors?

The Weeks to Come in the Hospital Rehab

Watching Bill lay in bed after having the stroke was so hard. I knew if I had tons of emotions going through my brain, he surely was overwhelmed with what-ifs, and why me? Although he never would actually cry, you could see he was holding it in. He constantly thanked me for my love and compassion and everything I did for him and apologized for everything he had done in the past. I know remorse was running through his veins and his heart, but I would imagine that this is what everyone does when all they do is lay there wondering what the future holds.

I was the frequent and steady visitor. I would do my best to come in the morning and at night, bringing the Bulletproof coffee and real eggs. Most of the time, I'd pack a lunch for him or go to the cafeteria and get a couple of sushi rolls and salad. At night, I would bring us both dinner; all he wanted was salmon, rice, and broccoli, but I brought it in hot, with real plates and silverware, and we ate together. After a while he let me mix it up, but very seldom did I ever miss dinner and we always ate together. I know many people thought I was killing myself and trying too hard to accommodate him, but if I were in his position, how would I want to be treated? I looked at it as the least I could do.

Seeing him all the time did get old, morning, noon, and night. I mean really, what do you talk about? News got old and controversial, he considered conversations about my work boring; fortunately, the family called him a lot and he did grandkid talk. He could not read, and he would fall asleep watching TV; I brought in the UNO card game and a deck of cards and revised the game, so he did not have to handle so many cards. I also made him a firm-foam wheelchair lap tray where he could hold his drink and cards between the foam. It put the competitive nature back in him and a level of concentration that he was missing. We also played dominoes and Fish. I left the games there in hopes his friends would want to play with him. His occupational therapists also had him playing with other patients, but from what I heard he was falling asleep too much.

I did call in the friends and family to please make some happy visits to break up his day and on weekends we had out of town guests. We did everything we could to be as normal and crazy as we all were. It made him so happy. Everyone knew to call me for his daily therapy schedule and come in when he was awake. It worked, but it was a schedule for me to keep up with. I had started a blog so anyone who needed to know what was going on could easily go there to see his day, instead of calling me. As we saw Bill's lack of strength to keep his eye lids open, we wrapped it up and left him to dream land.

Leg Spasms &
Bowel Movements

As previously noted, one of the biggest issues Bill faced in the hospital and nursing home was the drugs they gave him for his spasms. Everyone at the hospital and in rehab treated us like we were nuts when Bill complained of the severe and painful spasms he was having on his left side; after all, he was paralyzed and could not feel anything. He screamed with the pain, and I mean screamed out loud. They would give him all kinds of drugs to release the muscles, but the muscles would never really release. He still had the spasms; they would make him sleepy to the point where he would fall asleep all the time. He would have therapy scheduled and he would be unresponsive due to being drugged. He would ask that they not drug him because he wanted to do therapy, but then he would go to the therapy room and have excruciating spasms, and they could not do therapy.

My daughters and I researched stroke spasms and found we could buy a CBD cream that had a small amount of THC online. We also gave him additional Magnesium in a spray that we would put on the muscles, and we gave him CALM drink and Niteworks from Herbalife. This helped, but the doctor really frowned on outside cures and wanted us to keep with their care that was not working. Needless to say, we found our way to help him and did not allow him to have to scream for drugs to stop the pain. In our research, we found so little on the spasms and no one really addressed this as an issue with stroke patients, but as we talked to more patients, they all went through this and were still going through this years later. More on this later, we did find successful treatments.

When you have paralysis, you do not feel anything, not even pressure on that side. Did anyone ever think to mention to us that the intestines on the left side do not work either? Or, that you really do not feel the need to urinate until it is coming down the shoot? Everyone looked at us like we were out of our minds when he had a major need to have a bowel movement. They had kept him on a laxative and a stool softener, but when it is ready to come out, there is no warning until your right side feels either the pressure from the push on the left side or the surprise warmth in your bed. Then, when you ring your call button, it takes 3 to 4 minutes for them to come in to help. By then, your room smells into the hall and everyone is trying to clear the airwaves.

The CNAs would come in and clean him up, with his backside totally exposed to the elements. They'd do their best to dismiss the odor of stored-up fecal matter and spray the hall and room with a "Poop-be-Gone" spray that let everyone know you had just messed your bed. Any dignity Bill had was gone from the day he had the stroke. His butt was always in full view and his frontals were so exposed that it left nothing to the imagination. Like he said, "I never in a million years thought I would have beautiful young women caringly wash my jewels and not get excited." I lightheartedly told him, "Don't look at me to do that."

However, I have to say, pooping and spasms are the two hardest things to deal with after a stroke. This is where a good masseuse comes in; I would massage his leg and arm, and his large intestine, all the way to the shoot. I know that sounds gross, but if you tell them not to cut the cheese or pass the gas while you are massaging them, it is doable. I would follow the intestine from his right side where he had feeling, all the way across to the left side. Then I would flip him to his right side and do it again. This ended up becoming a ritual so he could be somewhat normal; after all, it was pushing the poop that gave him the stroke originally.

The bedpan ended up being the deadpan. He could not sit up in his bed with a pan stuck to his butt and poop. They'd leave him like that for an hour at a time until he'd wake up and ask to have it removed. At the hospital, they ended up putting the ol' commode next to his bed and lifting him onto the pot, or they would use a slide board to get him to the pot/commode. Once in a while, he would have success, but it was not something that worked well.

Previously while at the hospital, Bill had the most compassionate male CNA who was wonderful. Jason was so nice to Bill and moved him to a chair and wheelchair, unlike others who did not have the muscles he did. Bill and I convinced Jason to move Bill to the toilet, the real toilet, as in the porcelain throne. BAM! It was like a miracle, elation set in like a cure or a moment of hope and relief. I truly felt that Jason understood Bill and was in tune with his intestinal discomfort.

Without spending any more time on this subject, all I can say is, "Make it a priority" to help your patients get to a real toilet, it will mean the world to them. I know there is an issue with staff shortage and lack of qualified staff to move them, but I did it at home with a slide board. Caretakers need to understand, constipation and bowel movements are still a problem, and it will always be a problem; he cannot feel the movement until it travels down the shoot. Just know if Dulcolax and MiraLAX do not work and you are eating tons of broccoli and drinking water, on the 4th day of no results, drink half a bottle of Magnesium

Citrate and lots of water. It is the Liquid Plumber for your body's pipes. Be prepared with those tiny bubbles, they are usually a sign of what is to come.

I learned the hard way. When you need to put protection on your spouse, never refer to it as a diaper or pamper, it is a "brief." Kids who find out their parent or grandparent is wearing a diaper think it is hilarious and have no problem blurting it out in public. "Grandpa wears diapers" hahaha or when you are in a store, "Hey Grandpa, do you need any diapers?" The kids were little and full of humiliating humor, and we had a great laugh, but Grandpa did not think it was funny.

See more about this issue while at the Nursing Home later in this book.

Care: What Works and What Doesn't

I would like to spend more time on the use of acupuncture and TENS, but both the hospital and the nursing home insisted we not use this treatment because of his defibrillator and their scheduled treatments. I am a true believer in acupuncture treatments and so is Bill, but I cannot say too much as I had to stop his treatments.

In my weekly hospital meetings with the social workers, doctors, and rehab, I never felt like I was getting a favorable report. They would try and outline what Bill's and my expectations should be, and what the staff would be doing for him the next week. If I was traveling that week, and missed the Friday meeting, I would do it by phone or catch bits and pieces when I returned. It had seemed to me that they did not appreciate it if I had viable questions about his care or his progress.

To me, all of this was such a downer. I never felt invigorated to push harder, to seek alternative treatments, or to get more involved with his care. All I got from the meetings was to be prepared for him to never walk again, that he would need constant care, think about quitting my job to stay home with him and do his care, sell my house, and move into a ranch-style house or assisted living or keep him in a nursing home for the rest of his life. Wow! What options! In other words, this is it, you are now going to live this new life, accept it. I had said earlier that I am a strong woman and I do not take "no" for an answer and I will not accept defeat. I do not remember my words to them, but they knew I was not going to quit, and they did not approve of my demeanor. From what I heard; I was the talk of the floor.

Thanksgiving was days later, and I had reserved one of the therapy rooms to bring in the meal and family so we could all enjoy the day together and Bill could get out of his room. We all did so well, and Danielle and her family helped to cook and carry it all in. Bill was so happy everyone was there and that we did this for him. The staff were not as pleased, but they accepted our family time. I am sure they did not want to be there on Thanksgiving either. They had all gotten used to me bringing in his own food and not eating hospital food like everyone else.

We wore him out fast and recognized his stamina was not what it used to be. You can see in the photos, we had to strap him into his chair all the time, otherwise he would be on the floor. How he loved having us all there and not missing one of his favorite meals: Thanksgiving Chicken! And sweet potato with pecans and marshmallow casserole

A couple of days later we all came back in with another dinner and tres leche cake to celebrate Xavier's birthday. Even I ate this cake. Now it was time to fast for two weeks before Christmas.

Days later they called me in to say Bill would be transferred over to a nursing home and I should go around and find one I liked. I was leaving the next Monday on a business trip and would not be back until Thursday. That afternoon at my lunch hour I went to 3 of the nursing homes that were on their list. Have you ever lost it in front of people who are trying to be nice? I remember that entire day I cried as I went from home to home looking for the best place for him. The one I really wanted him to go to that was on the hospital's recommended list could not take him, he required too much care and rehab. and they could only do so much. Then another one on the list had rehab, but it was for older people, and it was located in their lunchroom where they were serving hot dogs and potato chips for lunch. I went with the third one on the list, their rehab was newer, more focused, and closer to home. What did bother me was the nursing home for the geriatric patients was right with the rehab patients, but I had to overlook some things and accept the good.

On to the Rehab Nursing Home

I was on the planned work trip and got the call from the social worker that they would be releasing Bill from the hospital and that I had 48 hours to tell them where I was to have him transferred. I had only spent an hour and a half looking at these rehab nursing homes, I needed more time. Sorry, he has to be out of here by Nov. 31st. Everything I had previously read said that he had 5 to 6 weeks at the hospital rehab, "why are you releasing him after only 3 weeks?" Are you ready for this one? They said, "He could not stay awake during his rehab, so they were not able to treat him anymore." I commented, "But you give him too many drugs for his spasms, it is not his fault he cannot stay awake!"

Needless to say, I was talking to a wall, and he was out of there. I gave them my 1st and 2nd choices and they had to go with my 2nd choice because of Bill's level of stroke severity and heart condition; he would have been too much for them to handle. I did not have the option to look at more facilities, between the quick lunch trip to see the homes and my work travel, it left me with no time.

We went with Genesis, which was 4.5 miles from the house. Everyone was so kind and so accommodating; they knew my level of anxiety and wanted to make me confident in their services and convince me they would do what they could for Bill. I am sure we gave them a lot of first-time issues, but they did what they could to help him. I really do not think there is any facility that can treat the individual needs of every patient, but they tried, which helped to make his stay more palatable.

First, Bill is tall, good-looking, happy, and has a great personality. He has his way with women and does well conveying nice thoughts. However, if he has a problem, he holds it in; take for instance, his 6'5" frame did not fit the bed, or he was constipated, or he was in severe pain with spasms; he would rather that you see his predicament and come to him with a solution without him saying a thing. He will groan and moan or wince aloud, but he will not say, "I am constipated." After 44 years of marriage, I can say, "I know this man well."

Men who are 6'5" do not fit in hospital beds, period! He had to constantly use his right foot and right arm to pull himself up higher in the bed. It would take 2 CNAs to pull him up in bed about 10 times a day. With his spasms, he was constantly going deep to the bottom of the bed, but worse, he was rubbing the back of his paralyzed ankle at the Achilles tendon and the shin raw to the muscle. They would bandage him up, but he would rub it off with the constant movements of the spasms.

They literally tried everything, but he thrashed so much it wore everything off. After a week or so, it got infected and they ended up having to change his dressing 2 to 3 times a day to ward off infections and keep it from bleeding, while also making the bandage indestructible. This lasted for over 5 weeks until they could get his leg to calm down.

Then they brought him in an airbed that extended the bed and kept him from inching down to the bottom of the bed. It was the answer, but the constant run of the loud motor annoyed him. He learned to live with it but hated the air mattress. Eventually, they brought in a long bed. I am sure all of his constant needs were a drain on the staff, but they did their best. They even went so far as to keep the room with only one patient. Can you imagine how bad it would have been if someone had to live with his constant needs? They really understood how no roommate would be happy to have to be crowded with Bill's level of care. I thanked them profusely for being sensitive to his high level of care.

The rehab at this facility was one of the better ones around. However, I do not think they were prepared for Bill, and I do not know how many facilities would actually be prepared. He showed such determination and commitment to recovering and gaining strength that he was begging for more time in the rehab room. Medicare only allows so much billable hours in a day; the rest is up to the generosity of the therapists. However, with all the patients they had to care for, they had to comply with the mandated schedule and put him back in his room. After a while, they could see he was not going to take "No" as an answer. After they were done with his allotted time, they would allow him to work at the occupational therapy table with squeezing or moving objects to wake up his paralyzed side.

Flint Rehab

No one at either rehab facility had ever heard of Flint Rehab until my daughters discovered it during their research. It was one of the best finds we had come across and we used almost every tool they offered or suggested to try.

This free online servicure is for stroke victims, hemorrhagic or blood-clot; it became our textbook and bible of strokes, and it trained us as caretakers on how to use tools and exercises to improve our patient's ability to make forward strides. Just listening to the various testimonials helped both Bill and me have hope; it gave Bill the fight he needed to keep going strong and not give up. I wish we had found this earlier in our research and I wish we had just invested earlier in all of the tools they offered to train with. If wishes were fishes, we'd all have many.

One of the tools we used immediately was the mirror therapy. My daughter built it with an inexpensive mirror inside a box. You put your paralyzed hand outside of the box and the good hand inside. As you move your good hand in the box, your paralyzed hand is moving in conjunction with the hidden hand. It was remarkable to see his paralyzed hand actually move, after all, it was paralyzed. We left the mirror therapy with the rehab facility; I hope they continued to use it with others.

There is also a music glove that teaches your brain to work with the computer program and your finger glove to move your fingers in coordination with what is being directed on the screen and make music. Bill was fascinated by his ability to have control and the progress he made. To this day he still uses it as it really helps with your coordination and touching your fingers to your thumb.

There are so many more tools they offered, like exercises, treatments, mental games, etc. I highly recommend this site and encourage everyone to allow them to send you the weekly exercises and video testimonials. Oh, did I tell you it was free? Only the tools cost money and it is not that outrageous. www.flintrehab.com

Money Money Money…..

I wish I could share with everyone the heartache I went through with money and finances. Much of what happened to us was from poor planning and misappropriation of funds. This is not a tell-all story, but I can say that the financial situation I found us in was almost equal to the pain of what I was going through with Bill.

When I cried all the time, it was mostly crying about "what am I going to do now?" Remember the ID and Password ordeal I went through in the Trauma Room in the ER? That night, I went home to see what we owed right away so I could pay the bills. Nothing made sense to me. Since I was working, I had stayed away from our finances and had allowed Bill to take care of everything. He and I have very different ways of money management and his way was not my way.

I do not want to portray myself as anal and in total control of every cent, but I do want to know where every cent of my money was going. I ended up letting him know what I had discovered; I know he was so hurt that I had determined the severity of our financials and that I had to share it with the family because I needed help sorting it all out. All I can say is I tackled it and did it, paying off everything I could and simplifying our lifestyle to afford our newest expenses.

After I had completed my initial list of accounts and bills to pay, I went to an Elder Care Lawyer feeling I should look into going bankrupt. Bill was a veteran, so they offered a half-hour for free. After my first discussion, I paid for an additional hour. This gave me the peace of mind that I did not need to go bankrupt and let me know that everything was going to be OK. From there I put together a schedule to pay everything off within 18 months. It was a relief to know that I was going to be OK and I did not have to negotiate the cards down or refinance. I was so proud of myself for taking the bull by the horns and getting it done.

Bill's medical bills for the past 12 years had amounted to over $220,000 and we were expected to pay them off. Bill had played into the 0% transfer credit card game, moving money for 12 years, but it hardly made a dent in what was owed. Living in a small state like Rhode Island, and the care we had was not for out-of-state incidents, so insurance only covered 20% of the adjusted cost of his 21-day stay in 1986 in the Intensive Cardiac Care Unit at NY Columbia Presbyterian Hospital. Lessons learned are very costly. Healthcare for those who are working and paying their own way is not cheap. For me alone under Obama Care was $960 a month. I could not wait to grow old and go on Medicare. Now under Medicare, we each pay about $360 a month for our supplemental and what is deducted from our Social Security checks.

One of the suggestions Elder Care had recommended was sharing all of my information with my daughters, giving them passwords, account numbers, monthly costs, and due dates. I have as much as I can on autopay and what is not on autopay, I write the check. I also found out that Bill should not be on any of my accounts and should not be a beneficiary of any policy or account. Bill needs to go through a 5-year plan with no money in his accounts, then he can go on Medicaid if necessary. In the event I cannot care for him anymore, he can go into an adult living center, and it would be covered by his Social Security check.

The VA adult living center may be an option in the event I cannot lift him anymore.

Having talked to many wives & caretakers who have discovered many of the same issues, I was not alone. I also found that this holds true in families that have not been afflicted with a trauma, so many women do not get into the details of their personal finances because their husbands let them know they have it all under control. Men find this out too; their wives can be in control of the finances and husbands just take for granted everything is OK. My financial planner went into so many stories of despair. I found out that this is oftentimes why people rely on a Financial Advisor to help them through hard times.

I encourage everyone to put every cent you spend on a spreadsheet; write out all of your account numbers and data in one place with phone numbers; know all of your accessible funds in the event you need them, and keep your IDs and Passwords hidden someplace private. Keep your wills, your Declarations of Care, your insurance policies, and just absolutely everything in one file and scanned into your computer. When it comes to Tax Day, I have everything on my spreadsheet and all I have to do is copy the numbers over. It makes life so much easier.

Give at least two of your family members access so they can get to something if you cannot. I am so organized now that I feel so calm if anything should ever happen again. It was so therapeutic to get this done and it is a weight that has been lifted off my shoulders. Even my financial planner was thrilled to see how I had done so much on my own, and our CPA said what I had done made it so much easier to do our taxes.

No one can ever prepare you for the shock of taking control of your entire household, another person's full-time care, working full-time, money management, and taxes. I listened to the radio in the car all the time, especially talk shows. This one day they had a team talking about managing your finances and planning for your future. Everything they were talking about was about me; it was like they knew my story. I listened to them a few more times and then decided to make an appointment.

I already had a great financial planner, and he was doing a good job, but I needed better planning. I needed control and, right then, I needed handholding. I did pass all of our investments to a local planner and have since worked to build my assets to the point where every bill was paid off within a year and I am able to retire if I have to. But…. I do not want to; I want to continue to work. It is my outlet.

Buy a Scanner or use your smart phone and scan everything, I do mean everything. Get 2 notebooks and keep one with the patient and one with you. Bill wrote what he could, but he would have the CNAs, or his guests help him if I was not there. Anyone who came to see him, any news, and whatever they were going to schedule.

Things you would never think about scanning were driver's license, insurance cards, VA card, Military discharge papers, life insurance, your living will, your DNR, list of drugs and dosage, health insurance, and the list goes on. If I got a bill, I scanned it. If I got a report, I scanned and dated it as I did it so I could reference it later.

While money is "the root of all evil", however, without money, it is hard to accomplish what you need to get through and complete everything. Taking care of the costs of your spouse and opting to shoot the wad if you have to, can cost you more than you'd planned and more than you can get from Medicare. I will be touching on the costs later in my story, but know that with creativity and fortitude, you can do everything.

45-Days After The Stroke

It was now Christmas 2017, Bill was still in the rehab nursing home. The staff had nicely decorated the facility and made it festive for the patients. It goes without saying that Bill's room was decorated as much as I could without going overboard. Our daughter in NYC, her husband, and two kids were regulars every weekend, but what was exciting was that our other daughter, Gabrielle, Rick, our son-in-law, and two kids were flying in from Los Angeles for Christmas. This was not planned, but we all knew this was an important family time needed for all of us. Gabrielle had been doing Facetime with Bill, but there was a need to see him up close.

Danielle and her family had come up almost every weekend from New York City and she had been relaying to Gabrielle to keep her in touch. Having the entire family there was so important to Bill and made him feel whole. The staff was really accommodating and let us use a large portion of the dining area to allow us to set up meals and all eat together. Every day we had dinner as a family with the food we would bring in. We'd put the tables together and would have a normal, loud, and crazy dinner with real plates and metal silverware, talking like we would if we were at home. You could see Bill come alive; it was what he needed.

On Christmas, we waited for the dining room to become available, and we brought in the gifts for him and the gifts we as "Mom & Dad" were giving to the kids. The staff would walk by and check on us with huge smiles, you could see they were so happy for him. Every night after dinner, we broke out the games. Between UNO, card games, dominos, and hearty laughter from playing Ellen DeGeneres' game which is a phone app, "What's UP", we kept everyone entertained. Bill was so happy, and the staff were amused by our ability to have a good time and not treat Bill as the stroke victim. We did this every night for 6 nights and no one said, "No, not again."

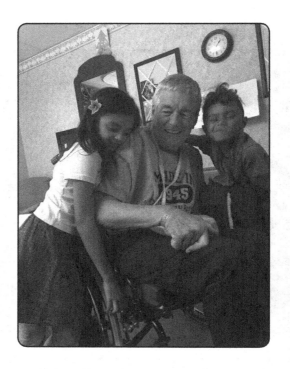

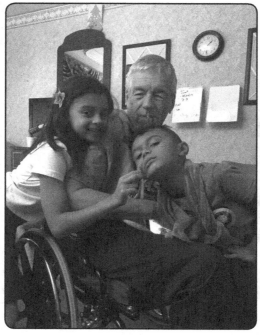

We took so many pictures and we created so many great memories, it gave Bill so much to remember and process later into his care. I must admit, we took a ton of pictures, and we created our own memories. We made a bad situation fun, and it did not cost us a dime.

After Christmas and the New Year celebration, it was back to normal life, no more decorations, cookies, candy, or big family parties. For anyone, it is a letdown, but for Bill, it was an even bigger letdown. Winter had set in; lots of snow outside, it was cold, and life had slowed down, even his brain's desire to train slowed. We had to pick up the pace, get back into the swing, and keep the momentum going.

His hair had grown so long, he looked like a beatnik. I washed his hair with cups of water, shampoo and a basin and went to town with the scissors. I brought towels from home and placed them all around to collect the cuttings. Then I gathered them all up and went outside to shake them out in the freezing cold newly fallen snow and shook them clean, only to have the wind pick up at that exact moment and left me covered in frozen gray hair from head to toe. I cursed until I was cursed; I looked up to the sky and said "Really? You had to blow wind at that exact time?"

It was time to get both of us, but especially him out of the joint for a night out for dinner. Our best friends from Connecticut were in town and we got permission to take him out for a few hours. I brought his coat and warms clothes, boots, and hat, bundled him up like a snow man, slid him into the wheelchair, got him into the front seat and off we went. We took him to our favorite sushi restaurant in the freezing cold snow, no one was out that night, it was way too cold to venture out. The venture to the table and sliding him onto the chair was such a great experience for him. You have to remember; it is the little things that bring so many great memories. He smiled from ear to ear and managed to handle the chop sticks with his right hand. It was the best thing for him. He still talks about it to this day.

Putting on the Pressure

While still at the nursing home, I saw the swing going downhill, he needed a jump-start. I remember sitting in his room at the nursing home one Sunday. We had just watched the Patriots' game on TV and we covered the portable potty chair and used it as a table for our snacks; this covered Potty Chair had been in his room since day one, but he had never used it. We had been talking about losing his dignity and how the biggest conversations we had were about his constipation and the fact that he was still on the bedpan, and nothing was working.

I went down the hall and asked if we could talk to the social worker who was on duty. That poor woman had no idea what I wanted from her, but I know she had not expected this. I explained how "My husband has lost his dignity; he has to continue to pee into a urinal, poop into a bedpan, and sit in bed waiting long stretches of time for help in removing the pan or urinal. He sits there in this bed and stares at the portable potty 24 hours a day and never gets to use it. The only thing we have used it for is a table for snacks while we watch football. I want him sitting on that chair from now on and I want him starting today!" She stood there cross-armed holding her folders, took a deep breath, and said, "Let me look into it." The very next day, he was sitting on the poop pot when he needed to poop, and his urinal was removed more often.

I then pushed the great people in rehab, asking them to do more with him and work him harder. They explained that Medicare only allows 1-hour of physical therapy and 1-hour of occupational a day. It meant nothing to Medicare that there were 22 more hours in a day, and he needed to do something more with his time.

With our persistence and with the great staff, especially Michelle, Cheryl, and Rob, they would leave him in the therapy room and allow him to use whatever he wanted to use on his own, as long as they were not using it. They also worked hard to get him to stand and sit and then later walk a few steps with a walker. You could see how they were taking his care personally and anything he achieved was because he had the drive to improve, and they had the drive to make it happen. He was so excited; he could not wait for me to see his advancements when I returned from my trip.

Medicare vs. Medicaid

If ever life was not fair, this is where it begins. You both work hard all your life, scrimp and save, you put money away for retirement, for your kids' schooling, weddings, vacations, house, etc.; you are a responsible, self-reliant taxpayer and you have never taken a dime for help. Then you go through the full description of Medicare vs. Medicaid, and you ask yourself, "What did I do wrong?" Should I have never worked hard? Should have never gone to college. Should have never saved for retirement. We were damned! We did everything we were supposed to do but we were not eligible for squat! However, if we had not been so responsible for ourselves and saved, we could have been on Medicaid and had everything for free! I would not have to pay for homecare or wheelchair services to drive to his twice-weekly therapy 30 minutes away or care for him when I am traveling. It would have all been free.

I really want to touch on this in more detail, so I have saved the particulars for later in the book. There is so much to learn about Medicare and Medicaid, and it was impossible to find real detailed information that was easy to understand.

At this point it is best to get as much help as possible from anyone who will offer it for free. Our insurance provider did try to help me, but at that point in time, I was so overloaded with information that I was not comprehending much of what was said. Going to the VA was the answer for me, and finding an advocate that could talk my language and appreciate my conflicts.

Nursing Homes, Veteran's Homes and VA Programs

My husband is a Vietnam Veteran. He proudly served as an officer in the Navy as a Navigator on a Destroyer in the Pacific until the end of the war. After graduating from Stanford, he enlisted in the Navy where he ended up in Newport, RI at OCS (Officers Candidate School). Now we live here in RI, right where he started, and have access to great VA care. Bill had already registered with the VA Hospital here in RI and used their care for a few things, so he was somewhat eligible for services, but I had no idea what he could get.

An advocate from the VA came to the nursing home and sat down with both of us and let us know what we were eligible for from the Government and VA. I could not believe how just his 2-hours of being with us lifted my emotions to the level of gratitude for the military and I appreciated all he and the VA were willing to do for us. I would push anyone to this assistance as soon as you can in the very beginning of your impairment.

I will get more into this later in the book, but it is important for everyone to know that the Government and the VA are very helpful and are a great source for your supplies and care.

Through all of this, I was traveling for my job and maintaining the house. Friends were great, visiting him all the time and our very close friends, Nancy & John, came from Connecticut almost every weekend to help out. Local friends and church friends came in all the time to see Bill and make sure he was staying motivated while I was gone. I would always let everyone know when I was taking off so they would go see him and bring him more nuts and dark chocolates.

When I returned after a long business trip, social services asked us for our weekly meeting. This time it was to tell me that Bill's time there was ending, and he would have to move out. They did not give me an exact date, but probably in 2 more weeks. They knew I had put off the inevitable and were concerned I had not made progress in finding an alternative to his need for care. I explained that I did not have the finances to do much of anything that I had hoped.

That is not how the system works. They wanted to allow Bill an additional month of nursing home care in the event he has another episode, but Medicare only allows you 90 days total every year. I then called the hospital asking if Bill could come back to the hospital and use the other 3 weeks, he had left that they had told me about. Their response was "No, we cannot do that, he cannot stay awake, and we cannot bring him back." They had also found out from the Nursing Home staff that I was sending him out to our daughter's house in California, where he could live in a single-floor house, and she could take care of him.

RI Hospital and the Nursing Home were definitely disappointed with me sending him to California. From then on, I am sure I was the main topic of conversation, "How dare she shun her wifely duties on to her kids!" But how was I ever going to be able to do this all by myself with no one to take care of him at home unless I paid for it?

The Cost of Home Care

No one can prepare you for the cost of home care. I would have to have a full-time CNA, or an experienced, strong caretaker come and live with us. If I were to use an agency, I would be paying $35 an hour. If I were to hire my own, it would be $22 an hour. If I am gone for 4-days, it would cost me $2,112 a week out of pocket. I would need to also pay expenses and travel to his many doctor's appointments. However, if he were on Medicaid he could have the care for free…. yes free! Ask me why I am working and busting my @$$ to be responsible and self-reliant? Yes, there is Long Term Care (LTC) insurance that we never purchased. By the time the kids got out of college, and we had to save for retirement, LTC was out of our budget. Now that I have talked to more people about this, they had this plan through their work benefits and very few had ever bought it on their own. Nursing homes are a minimum of $4500 a month, and that is for the VERY VERY low end. A medium care facility is around $6,500 and the one we all want to stay in is $8,500. When LTC only pays $4,500 a month, you need to come up with the balance. Now I can see why many people bring their parents home to live and find a way to make it work.

Elder Care Support

I also re-wrote our wills so that our daughters would be the beneficiaries in the event I passed first. They would be in charge of his care, and they would need the money for his expenses. They had also agreed to split his care, giving each other breaks and using the money for either day care or home care or even Adult Living Center Care. I also had a Power of Attorney written where I could sign Bill's name to anything in the event he was not capable. I did all of these forms online and then had the bank notarize them, saving a bundle in lawyers' fees. Five years later we did go to another Eldercare attorney where we had a more formal arrangement made with legal ease and formalities to secure our estate and not create a mess for our family to work through. It was surprising to find out how our kids were going to be taxed to death just to inherit our estate, and all I had wanted to do was make it a gift of love and happiness in their future.

Never, ever, think you are saving anything by doing it yourself with the online do-it-yourself forms; what I was saving was actually costing my family more in the end. Maybe probate would have held the estate over long enough to make it easier, but the idea was to simplify the care and finances for the family to take care of us. I also made it so the attorney is the executer so everything is done right away and fairly. I know it cost me more, but time is of the essence and the undue stress is not worth the headache it would have created.

Moving Home

They gave me 2 weeks' notice and asked that I prepare my home so he could see what it was like living at home, even though he was already scheduled to go to California. Yes, I cried, I panicked, and I lost my composure on many occasions. I had no idea how I was going to make it through all of this, but with the help of the good Lord and my friends and family, I got it done.

I found out that Medicare was going to give him his very own wheelchair. When they delivered it to the nursing home and put him in it, the chair fell back. There were no supports on the back to keep the chair from falling back. When he sat in the chair, his tall knees were under his chin; this was not a chair for a 6'5" person. Rob, at the Genesis Rehab immediately called Medicare to get a new one, and they said there is only one chair we offer, the basic chair. Rob then called the VA and found out he was eligible for a chair that would fit his tall frame and have the back supports so the chair would not fall back; he ordered it right away and had it sent to the house. I tried to return the Medicare chair knowing I would not use it; they informed me I had already paid for it and it was mine. What? I paid for this awful wheelchair, and I had to pay for it?

I also went to the local chapter of the Mason's where they offer free handicapped items. They loan the items that have been donated to them from private users; I got a beautiful, almost brand-new plush recliner chair that would lift him to a standing position or have him lay flat and sleep. They also loaned me this heavy motorized chair that had right arm controls. My neighbors, Ray & Mary, drove me over with their truck and helped me to get everything to the house in the driving snowstorm. I had to call in the cavalry to get the items up the stairs; it took 5-people to hoist the motorized chair up a bunch of boards improvised as a ramp to the first floor; I did not try to get it up one more to the 3rd floor.

My really close friend and her husband were "all there" for me, "What do you need? We will do it." When people are so nice you get super emotional, and you cry a lot out of gratitude. Marilyn and her husband, Tim, went all out. Tim was a Vietnam Vet who had been exposed heavily to Agent Orange in Vietnam and had a non-treatable form of cancer that left his leg in a boot-cast so he would not break it anymore. His body was full of cancer and his leg was the only visible sign. He was doing everything he could to live life and be normal. He brought over his tool kit and bolted in all 5 of my grab bars, climbing all of my stairs like he was normal. He later passed away from his Agent Orange cancer.

Our 4-story house is located on Narragansett Bay on stilts. It was a money pit that was our baby & forever project; now, our baby was going to need adjustments to adapt to ol' grandpa. I had many companies come in and discuss the elevators and stair chairs, ramps, lifts, and electric pullies. At this point, Bill was in a wheelchair, there was no walking or standing on his own. Moving him was with the use of a simple slide board that I would have to push under his butt and then lift him to the slide and get him into the wheelchair.

Before he came home, I did not know if he could use the stair chair or if I had to get him an elevator. Either situation cost money and I was still flat broke. I looked at all possibilities of an elevator so I would not have to transfer him in and out to the chair; the only place the elevator was going to work was if we put it outside. Winters can be very harsh here and I just could not do it.

A very compassionate owner of the company, Aid 4 Mobility, recognized my predicament, understood what I was going through, and worked out a deal for me. I put down a deposit and paid for the installation and then I would pay rent to him for the use of the 2 lift chairs for a year. If in the meantime, if I found Bill could not use the chairs, they would remove them and put in the elevator and use that money towards the cost of the elevator. It was the best solution, and they were the best company and had the best people to work with. Yes, I had a monthly payment, but it worked, and now I own it.

When I had gone to the Mason's the week before to get him all his wheelchairs, I felt greedy to need so many. One to take him from the car to the stair-glide chair, I used the motor chair on the 2nd floor, and I needed another one for the 3rd floor. Forget the 4th floor, he did not need to go there. But I also needed a light transport one for the car; wheelchairs are so heavy, I needed an easy-fold lightweight transport chair. The Mason's came through again!

The day had come, and Bill was to come home. I packed up his room, loaded the car, and left him there to have the handicapped van bring him home on a gurney. No, I could not drive him home in my car and no, it was not free. It was mandatory that I use this service and I had to pay for two people to bring him home and get him up one-flight of stairs on the stair glide chair. I paid $560 out-of-pocket for two people to bring him home from 4.5 miles away on a gurney. However, the next day I had to take him by myself in my car to his hospital appointment with the stroke doctor….and they were not paying me. Does anything make sense to you?

He was so happy to be home; it was a good feeling for him, and it meant the world to him that he had made this transition. I had made a nice wood-fire and a chicken dinner.

Nighttime had come fast, and he was exhausted, he wanted to go to bed. I managed to do the slide board transfer over to the stair-glide chair, strap him in, get him down the stairs, slide board transfer him again to the motorized wheelchair, transfer him again to the toilet, then transfer him again to the chair, and then to the bed. I undressed him for bed, pushed him to the center of our king-sized bed, kissed him goodnight, and then went upstairs to clean up, breathe, stretch, breathe, stretch, and then turn out the lights and go to bed.

As I lay there next to him, his paralyzed leg started spasming and flipping all over the place. I got up, sprayed magnesium on his entire leg, massaged him, gave him Niteworksâ by Herbalifeä, and went back to bed. The leg started in again, the spasms got even worse, I said, "Can't you just try and hold your leg still a little bit?"

In disgust, he said, "Don't you understand, I have no control and the leg just does whatever it does, I don't like it any more than you do."

I was doing my best to sleep and an hour later I heard, "BAM!" His leg had fallen off the bed and onto the floor. He was struggling to stay in bed, saying "Help me, I am going to fall out of bed."

I quickly ran to the other side of the bed and lifted this 50 lb. dead-weight leg back up into the bed. I pushed him back into the center of the bed, jumped back into the bed, and tried to go back to sleep, but his leg continued to spasm. It was like he was possessed; this leg was all over the place! Then "BAM!" it fell to the floor again! I got up half asleep and put the 50 lb. leg back into bed, pushed him over to the center, and climbed back into bed.

Then "Bam!" it happened again! I got up and went over to pick up this #$% leg again and I slipped and fell into a pool of blood. He had slammed his leg into the dresser knob and gashed it really badly, there was so much blood all over the bed sheets, on the comforter, and on the floor, and now me! Have you ever been so tired and so exhausted that you cannot control your body and what comes out of your mouth? That was me!

I spent about an hour cleaning out his gash and blood, wrapped and bandaged his cut up to stop the bleeding, put his leg back in the bloody bed, cleaned up the floor, pushed him back in the center of the bed, and said, "I am out of here! I need my sleep! I am going to the day bed out in the other room and if you fall out of bed, I will take care of you in the morning when I wake up, you will be just fine on the floor."

I felt really bad for what I had said, but I had gotten to the point where my body could not do anymore, and my body had to sleep. He did sleep the rest of the morning and he never lost his leg off the side of the bed again. Cleaning up the room and washing everything the next day was just one of the many things I had to do, but to this day, I still find blood somewhere from that night.

Everyone was so kind, calling me to see how we were doing on our first day at home and his first night. My sister, Debi, heard the stress in my voice and went on Amazon and ordered a bed rail that I could install into the side of the bed, keeping Bill from falling out. Bill's friend, Lonnie, came over the next day to put it together and install it.

The first day home I had to take him to three appointments. The nursing home had set these up knowing he had to get the visits done before he went to California. The first full day at home I did 42 transfers. I know that does not sound like much, but for a 66-year-old, it is a lot. This meant I had to take him in and out of the car 3 times, in and out of bed and to the toilet umpteen times, into his stair-glide chair, up and down, into his recliner, and God knows how many more places.

My back was done! That slide board was not easy! And my patience had reached the point of no return. I had only dropped him twice that day. The one time from the recliner to his wheelchair when the board was not completely under him, and the board bent and down he went. I had to call the EMTs, and they came with such nice smiles and understanding and lifted him back up into the wheelchair.

The other time I was taking him to his PCP, parked in the handicapped spot, and tried to stand him up, and down he went onto the asphalt. Fortunately, a guy came and helped me to lift him into his chair. But, twice in one day, with 42 transfers, that's not bad for a first full day.

Things never got easier when he was home for the 7-days. EMTs only had to come to the house one more time to pick him up off the ground from the top of the stairs when we missed the stair chair, and friends had been so kind to come over with lighthearted conversations. Every day I took him to an appointment and every day I cried and cried and cried. This was not easy for either one of us, but I really wanted to make this work.

The nursing staff came once a day to make sure he got his sponge bath and changed his briefs (aka Pampers) and clothes, took his vitals, and made sure I had not gone off the deep end. They were all concerned that this was not going to work out and that I was not capable of caring for him in this 4-story house.

Bill's Move to Los Angeles

Bill's trip to California was not until Feb. 10th, my daughter's birthday. Happy Birthday, Gabrielle! Here is your present!

Danielle and my grandson, Xavier, accompanied Bill to California. Arriving a day before the trip, they could see this was not going to be easy, but they were prepared. I had packed him for 6 months with 2 large suitcases and a backpack full of all the things he would need on the trip. It took us two cars; my friend Tim came with his truck and put as much in the back as he could fit, and I took the rest in my car. He had a regular wheelchair, a transport wheelchair, a walker, cushions, armrests, 2 big suitcases, Danielle and Xavier's bags, and everyone's backpacks.

The first leg of their flight was from Providence to Newark, then they were to wait for 4 hours for their connection, a non-stop to Los Angeles. I had put on his brief, an extra pad, and a urinal in the event he did not make it to the toilet. They had landed in the A Terminal and walked around looking for a Family Restroom. They could not find anything. They asked around and were told to go to the C Terminal. After an hour they made it over there to the International Terminal and found the Family Restroom, but it was occupied.

Bill hung in there for a little bit longer and then let Danielle know he could not hold it in. About 20 minutes had passed and she started knocking and the guy inside said he would be right out. As he unlocks the door, Danielle recognizes that this is a nicely coiffed and impeccably dressed airline executive with a name tag that let Danielle know he was someone of importance. As Xavier pushed Bill into the room, Danielle went running off after this guy and lit into him with, "How dare you use this family restroom meant for handicapped people as your personal bathroom. My father had to go from......." The guy walked away with his tail between his legs and never apologized and never looked back. We tried to take the complaint to the top but never got anywhere.

Needless to say, Danielle and Xavier had to strip him down, clean him up, and use the spares I had packed. I have never been so proud of both my daughter and her then 14 Y/O grandson for just doing what they had to do and cleaning him up. It was their first time doing anything like this and they were my heroes. Try asking your kids or grandkids to clean you up after you have messed yourself up and see the resistance. Not these two, they just did it. This was their dad and grandpa and they loved him.

It was a long day for the family, taking over 12 hours to go from our house to my other daughter, Gabi's house, but they all made it safe and sound and loaded up 2 cars of family and their stuff. When he got there, he went to bed and didn't wake up until the next morning.

Next Steps Fitness Gym

Dancing with the Stars had a cute young contestant, Victoria Arlen, who was paralyzed on her entire left side, and she was competitively dancing on Dancing with the Stars and winning. Her story became a national phenomenon, between the television, newspapers, magazines, and the internet, her story was out there. At 11 years old, she had been afflicted with a disease that left her in a coma, paralyzed, and affected her brain; she lost her ability to walk. We searched her story and found her methods of success in walking were from a training the brain program in San Diego, that had also since closed. They also had a smaller place near Santa Monica. Her whole story can be read: https://people.com/tv/dwt-victoria-arlen-most-memorable-year/ & https://heavy.com/entertainment/2017/09/victoria-arlen-story-dancing-with-the-stars-paralympian-swimmer-dwts-2017/

With both places now closed, we found another facility close to my daughter's house that used much of the same practices that they used, and this facility had partial funding from the Christopher Reeves Foundation. Before Bill had gone out to LA, Gabi had looked into this to see if he was eligible and if they would accept him. I got all of his doctors to sign off on this: PCP, neurologist, cardiologist, physiatrist, and therapist all agreed he could participate. They accepted him into their program and the training began.

Next Steps Fitness is a fitness gym for people who have gone through spinal injuries; stroke victims were not often accepted into the program, but they appreciated Bill's desire to get better and walk so they took him in. They also liked the fact that he had once been an All-American Swimmer for Stanford and had the upper body strength to get through this. Janne Kouri, the founder of Next Steps Fitness had severed his spine when he dove into the surf and hit a sandbar at Santa Monica Pier. He wanted a place where he could go and workout daily and keep up with the locomotor training that he had learned at the many facilities post-injury. Janne, a business student graduate and MVP football player at Georgetown University, used his resources and knowledge to make it happen and build a gym. With the help of investors, his commitment, and the desire to get a facility up and running, he has dedicated his life to spinal injuries and training.

Here are a few of Next Step Fitness' accomplishments:

Since 2008, NextStep has been a resource to people and families globally, launched a nationwide movement, and inspired millions.

- Opened paralysis training centers in Los Angeles, Atlanta, Orlando, Kansas City, Raleigh, Phoenix, and Las Vegas (and now the Ukraine)
- 1st community-based center in the Reeve Foundation NeuroRecovery Network
- 1st community-based center to offer Locomotor Training in the US.
- Launched a nationwide movement - In NextStep's footsteps, 5 facilities have joined the NRN in Louisville, Salt Lake City, Minneapolis, Boston, and Chicago.

- Launched a movement in South Alberta through a medical community partnership to increase and improve services for those with paralysis.
- Awards: County of LA Access Award, Telly Award, and Classy Award Finalist
- National televised media coverage on CNN, ABC, CBS, HLN, Discovery, and more
- Launched Wounded Veterans Scholarship Fund and Quality of Life Grant and Low-Income Scholarship Programs
- Partnership with Revived Soldiers Ukraine to provide rehabilitation and fitness for wounded Ukrainian soldiers.
- Raised over $4,000,000 in support of people suffering from paralysis.
- Improved the quality of life, recovery, and overall health of over 2,000 individuals.
- Support 200+ individuals and their families on a monthly basis.
- With improved health and independence, NextStep members have been able to start new careers, go to school, start driving, get married, start families, and most of all, live healthy and happy lives.
- Internship programs and partnerships with universities across the country including; UCLA Cal State Dominguez Hills, Stony Brook University, and more.

Bill was so fortunate to get into this program and work with these people, I only wish there were more Next Steps around that were affordable like theirs was. Right away after Bill arrived in LA, he went to the facility and started his training. Gabi would pack him a salad for the day, granola bars, and pockets full of baby carrots. The team of trainers joked about how one day they were getting Bill on a machine and all these baby carrots fell out of his pockets. They all joked with him calling him out about eating rabbit food. He lunched and snacked with all the trainers and trainees and formed a real bond. It meant so much for him to be around others in similar situations and all able to have fun and joke about their situations. He looked forward to going there every day and would stay until someone could pick him up and take him home.

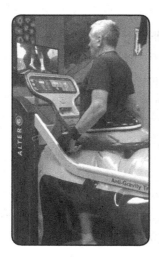

Bill hanging over the treadmill as they guide his legs in motion.

The machines they had there were designed for spinal injuries, and some were donated from NASA's weightless training. It was the best gym I had ever seen, and it is dedicated to getting paralyzed people to either walk on their own or walk with assistance. There are so many things you never think about, and people in wheelchairs or people who are paralyzed working out was one of those things until Bill was afflicted. Many of these people who work out at Next Steps gym were veterans, or former athletes who were accustomed to exercising in a gym. It does not seem right that all of a sudden, this activity stops.

He could go to the gym as much as he wanted to, but his specialized training was scheduled, and boy did they work him. If your training was for an hour or 2 hours, you did not give up.

Bill standing on his own for me....
I think he wanted a full frontal hug.

When I was there, they got him to stand from a sitting position and not hold on to anything. We all take this for granted, but for Bill, it was a HUGE accomplishment. All of these trainers were so dedicated and attentive to his advancements, it was so nice to see personal care and individual attention given to their clients.

Every day, they would share videos that they would take of him either walking in suspension or in an air-filled torso apparatus that allowed your feet to touch a moving treadmill. They would send me these videos to Rhode Island, and I would break down crying. There was hope and he was happier than I had seen him in months. I shared this video over and over again sharing my joy. I only wish there were more of these centers all over the place. https://www.nextstepfitness.org/

They do have 8 gyms located around the world and each one is different. I only know the one in Los Angeles, so I can only say to everyone that this gym is the best. If your paralyzed patient can move with another person to a location close to the gym and do this for 6 months, you will see a huge impact on improving their potential outcome. I recognize that this costs money and not everyone has access to the funds but recognize that I found a way and I was not in a good place financially. You have to find a way to give them hope and the drive to improve, and this was the BEST place I could have ever found.

Next Steps Fitness does not measure success by achievements they record in each individual, they feel everyone's injury and ability is different. They are not paying me to promote them, I am doing this on my own; so many have asked how to donate to them or how to get family into this facility.

If you go on to their site you will find many resources and links to various organizations and aids: https://www.nextstepfitness.org/goodinfo Use those links to the best information sources you can get to help with paralysis.

The links to resource articles are as follows:

Long-term exercise training in persons with spinal cord injury: effects on strength, arm ergometry performance and psychological well-being https://static1.squarespace.com/static/57aa517259cc6881bc278fab/t/5a8ced83e4966b93e392f1a6/1519185284437/Long+Term+Exercise+%26+SCI.pdf

Assessment of Functional Improvement Without Compensation Reduces Variability of Outcome Measures After Human Spinal Cord Injury

https://static1.squarespace.com/static/57aa517259cc6881bc278fab/t/5a8ceb1d9140b7d7d4b5a633/1519184670493/Assessment+of+Functional+Improvement+Without+Compensation.pdf

I did find another facility in Rancho Cucamonga, CA that was for stroke victims, however when I called them to discuss Bill, they gave me no hope and no options, and they were way overpriced. They would not work with me, and they offered me no alternatives.

Gabrielle's Training

My daughter, Gabi, is a personal trainer by trade and a Doctor of Chinese Medicine by training. She had more ways of working each part of his body than Bill wanted to know about. She put together a daily routine for him to do on the floor and couch. She taught him how to use a chair to get up from the floor, and a bunch of exercises to build his core. She's a tough one and would not allow him to say, "no more" and the kids stayed right with him counting to make sure he did them all. She has a business called "Body by Gabi" and works with all kinds of training needs in person and online; I would add "Stroke Training" to that too.

Gabi took Bill for short walks with his walker

The kids and I took time to laugh a little

She was dedicated to making sure that every penny I was spending to have him out there training was worth it. Her husband, Rick, also was a huge help lifting him to his chair and toilet and pushing him around, picking him up off the floor. He even showered him and helped him dress. It was a family of love. I know to this day that Bill and I are both so grateful to our daughters and the family who participated in his care. Bill needed a lot more care than I am writing about, but everyone was right there to help him.

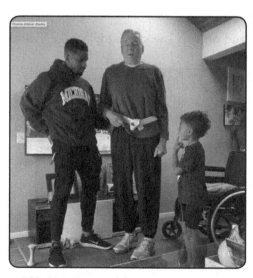

Rick would hold Bill up with his gate belt to practice standing

I did come out every month or so for a week, and I would try to give Gabi and Rick a break. I would drive him to his VA appointments and to his gym. I usually stayed with him the entire day and was able to see how much improvement was happening every month. His friends in California and our relatives would come and join us and go to lunch or just come and talk. You could see that he was alive again, and he was loving the warm California weather.

Months of Training: Including CBD & THC

Between Gabi's training and the training, he was getting from Next Steps, Bill was gaining strength and hope. This was so good for him. No one let up from the gas pedal and everyone gave him the support he needed to continue to work his brain and body. Gabi continued to introduce new methods and exercises and had him folding clothes, working with the kids; helping with their homework, reading to them at night, and some babysitting when the kids were in bed and asleep.

He was losing a lot of weight and gaining muscle, but the spasms were still an issue. She did lots of acupuncture, cupping, massaging, and remedies, but nothing worked quite like a cannabis gummy. After figuring out the right dosage, it became a nightly ritual and the really bad spasms were history. He still will have spasms, but nothing like the ones when you would think he was possessed. They kept it from me for a while, until I was there for my monthly visit and they referred to his nightly gummy. They thought I would be against it, but I was for anything that worked.

While in RI, we had achieved his status to have THC, so for those who were wondering, yes, we did go through the costly venture and doctor's approval. "We" had a background check done by the National Criminal Information Center (NCIC) from our local police department, got fingerprinted, and obtained a BCI report. I had to spend $100 (non-refundable) for me, the Caretaker, and another $100 for Bill. However, if we were on Medicaid, it would only be $25. There were other costs involved to get all of this done, but by the time I got everything, Bill was able to get whatever he wanted in California. Hence, I never finished my application. Now it is free and anyone can have it.

All of this was to see if we had any previous records. We were cleared and were allowed to be stoned legally. I do not want anyone to think you have to get high to the point where you are experiencing psychogenic dreams, but you need to be able to calm your nerves enough to relax the muscles. It does stop the spasms and you can sleep with the correct dosages.

I will admit, I tried it to see how it would affect me. I took a full gummy….WRONG! I should have only taken .25mg. You would laugh, but I went to bed right away and found my legs would not move and my body was flattened to the bed, I could not even roll over. Being that middle-aged woman who gets up nightly to relieve myself, I could not get out of bed. I kept on saying to myself, "Now what do I do? I am stuck here for the night!" Time passed, I fell back to sleep and the urge went away, but I will never forget the feeling.

CBD cream also works great, rubbing this on his leg in strategic places, not the entire leg, really does relieve the exact muscles that are cramping. Having Bill pointing to the place meant that I could help him more. I know there are so many people who are out there who are cautious to try these miracle methods, but take it from me, this is great stuff, and do not hesitate to try it.

I even make Bill his own gummies and I use them too. It allows him great REM sleep and he is fresh and strong in the morning. Take one box of sugar-free Jello, one pack of Gelatin, and 1 cup of boiling water and mix it together in a small square or rectangle glass container, then add 2 mg of CBD/THC drops cut it into 12 squares and take one at bedtime. If one does not do it, take another.

My Life in RI

I stayed busy keeping up with the house, working, traveling for work, Co-Chairing community fundraisers for our Church & Village, and continuing to work on our finances. As much as I did not mind being home all alone, I found I was not doing well. Once I had a chance to slow it down and work steadily on everything that "had-to-be" done (i.e. taxes), I buckled down and did it and completed it, but I got very depressed. I loved my 10 PM nightly Scotch so I could sleep and found it was my way of calming my nerves, but I knew I had to stop.

I went to my doctor, and she put me on an antidepressant, and I stopped drinking. I started to go back to the gym every night and walked every morning; I had to get myself back. I had shared this with a select few so they would know where my head was directed, and I stayed dedicated to being OK.

I had also been on a committee to find a new pastor for our church for the past couple of years. The long-drawn-out venture took us so much longer than we had planned, and we had to find someone "NOW." Having something so important to focus on was what I needed. While Bill was gone, we found our new pastor; I was so excited and happy to have found someone who was so important in our church life. It gave me purpose and a spring in my step, I could not wait for Bill to meet him when he would come home. I loved going to church and centering myself, it was where I could pray to God and thank him and all of my friends for their continued support. I am not an overly religious person, but I really thrive on fellowship and a sense of belonging. Our church was now complete, and I felt peace come over me.

Working full-time and traveling was really great for me. I could work hard and reap the benefits of my success financially. I got on a schedule and paid off everything, and still pay for all of Bill's therapy and training. I could also afford to share in the costs of keeping Bill fed and cared for. It was the best feeling. My customized spreadsheet was allowing me to realize I was going to be OK and my life was not going to fall apart.

I knew Bill's time in California was going to soon come to an end and I know it should have come to an end months before he actually came home. Ava wanted her bedroom back; Lennox wanted his room to himself without Ava, and Gabi and Rick needed their family back. Bill had started to get very short with the kids and yelled at them a little too much. He was not doing well mentally, and they had grown tired of him. The kids had expressed many times how they wanted him to go home, and that they did not like him anymore. Kids will be kids, especially when they are 5 & 6. It hurt him awfully, he never wanted it to come to this and he felt bad. Even with their family meetings and trying to work with Bill, he had gotten way too mean, demanding, and not fun to be with. He had lost his "happy."

Depression

Gabi had commented to him that he should go on antidepressants and not get so angry with the kids, but he was totally against this and did not think he was depressed. He knew I was taking pills, but he could see why I was depressed. Even though the two of us had gone through a psychologist at the VA in California, it was never prescribed or mentioned. Shortly after he got home, I took him to see his PCP. She was amazed to see how much he had improved and was absolutely thrilled with his successful training. When I brought up the idea of antidepressants for him, she said "Of course you should, heck I am on them…. How do you think I can take care of my kids, work full-time, be a good wife, keep up with my housewife stuff, and still be this happy doctor?" When he heard that he jumped at the chance to go on them. From then on, he stopped being so angry and did not break out with his loud disdain for everything. The kids now love him, they liked the new Grandpa, and he was so much easier to be around.

I have also learned that it is crucial to stay physically active, keeping a steady pace with your exercise, i.e., walking. I found out that if you are walking at a steady pace, you cannot cry and you cannot stay depressed. It was good for me all the time, but I also saw it was good for him. The more he stayed active, the nicer he was.

Coming Home to RI

I knew life was about to change, so I devoted all of my time for the next 2 months to his care and getting him reacquainted with the house and living in RI. It was the end of my bachelorette life and I needed to focus on him, not me. I was OK with this and looked forward to him coming home.

I did everything I could to take him wherever I could. It was so much easier to get him to stand up and sit down without too much help, get him up and down the stairs, and in and out of his wheelchair. The little walks with a walker were a welcome occasion. He had been walking with the walker in California, but very wobbly, short, short distances, but we found the more he did, the better he got.

I would pack picnics and take him for a car ride to Newport or Jamestown to watch the crashing waves and get him out into his wheelchair to eat lunch or dinner. We got very creative with our fun and decided it was good to do an adventure every day when we could, we even did the movies. I packed most of our meals and saved as much as I could not to spend on food; Besides, Bill was still into his very controlled food intake, and we were OK with this.

I went back to the VA to see what more they could offer me to make his life easier. They sent me a brand-new shiny red walker with a seat & carrier and extension for his tall body. It was perfect! They also sent me a new commode and shower seat; I was now prepared for his return. Then, I found out I would need another walker on wheels and two more pole walkers, so I got another wheeled walker from the VA and two pole walkers from the Mason's, and then I bought extenders to make them taller.

Bill returns to RI all tan from living in CA

Every doctor wanted to see him when we got home, and we went to them all. It was quite trying on both of us, but I knew we had to get this over with, so I bundled the appointments all as close as we could. But the one visit he really wanted to go to was the nursing home where he had done his rehab. It was his desire to walk into the building and surprise all of his rehab therapists with his ability to walk.

You could see the shock on everyone's faces when he walked in. First, they had never really seen him stand up tall, he was always bent over or sitting in his wheelchair. His 6'5" body was standing straight up, and he was shaven and had a haircut. The comments were from "OMG! Is that you Bill?", "You are such a handsome man, look at you, are you the same Bill that lived here so long?" to "OMG, let me call ___ and ___, they won't believe this." I know we were disturbing the time others were training, but we wanted to have the element of surprise. I was surprised to hear so many comments about me and how I looked and how they really did not think I was going to make it, but like they said, "You really did make it, congratulations."

No one could believe how Bill was walking short distances, and that he was actually out of a wheelchair standing tall without anyone holding on to him. I have to admit though, he was putting forth every ounce of stamina in his body to walk in and hold his body up straight. It was the most he had ever done, and he had something to prove to everyone; "He could do it and he did it."

We went home after that, and he went to bed around noon. He was exhausted, but he was so proud of proving everyone wrong and showing everyone what was possible when you commit yourself to making it. He did it!

He was so proud of himself that he wanted me to take him to the RI Hospital Rehab and show them his accomplishments and throw it back in their face how they had given up on the wrong person, but I asked that he wait until we had to go to the hospital for more tests and then go see them at the same time. This was the one place he wanted to go and express his disdain for the system and how they should change their program and minds. When he did go back, he hid his wheelchair, walked to the nurses' station, and asked them if they remembered him. The CNAs and therapists all came running over and showed absolute amazement and could not believe how great he looked and that he was walking so well. The doctors "did not" come out to see him, but they were there. The point he wanted to make was to show them he could do it and he did it, and they should have believed in him.

The Gym & Aquatics

Before Bill came home, I talked to the staff at our gym and discussed Bill in detail, knowing I was going to need assistance getting him around. I had explored several facilities within 1 hour of our house. The places that focused on rehab for spinal injuries and paralysis were $1,000 a week plus the cost of personal training. I would have to drive 1 hour each way and stay 2 hours, I really could not afford it and I could not give up 5 hours a day.

If we were on Medicaid, there were a lot more options open to his therapy, and most of it was in your home. Since we only had Medicare and a supplemental, I would have to take him ½ hour each way and stay for 3 hours. Our supplemental insurance policies did not cover anything except medicine.

The YMCA was an option with the Recumbent bike that is outfitted for paralyzed members. It was not the same bike that he was used to at Next Steps, so I opted to stick with our gym at LA Fitness. The staff had assured me they would help me any way they could, and they had a handicapped family room where I could change him. All I can say is, WOW! This staff and this gym were my saviors; our angels from heaven. They not only went the extra mile, but they also made it so I had no worries whatsoever.

When I would push his wheelchair up to the front door of the building, they would always immediately meet me at the door and open it, grab the wheelchair, and help me to push him through to the handicapped family room. They would allow me 15 minutes to change him and then push him through the Men's Locker Room to the pool. Two guys would then help me get him into the motorized pool chair that would lower him into the pool.

From there, I would hold up Bill until he got his footing and put him to the side of the pool where he could hold on with his right hand. In the beginning, it was kind of rough, but after the third time there, things got easier. His exercise was to practice lifting his left leg, and not dragging his foot, then he would need to lock his knee so he would not fall over. He would hold on to my hands and I would walk backward, repeating the words, "Lift", "Lock", "Lift", "Lock", "Lift", "Lock" …. for 45 minutes. Repeating these words eventually became embedded in his brain and he knew to do it on his own. It was so exciting for both of us knowing he could do this without too much handholding and bracing. This was the biggest real hope we had seen in a long time; we repeated this almost every day.

This facility was absolutely perfect for his needs. Their pool was never too deep, and they were so accommodating for anyone with a handicap. Angel, who was the gym manager, and Gavin, who was in charge of membership, took extra care to make sure Bill was taken care of. I was so blessed to have found such wonderful people.

You could see that the staff at LA Fitness was so excited, it was like this was their newfound friend and they all felt they had something to do with his success. As far as I was concerned, I could not have done it without their help. You could see the staff watching him from the windows, all wiping their tears and tracking his progress. Grown MEN with big muscles!

It warmed my heart every day that we went there; the members were so wrapped up with his recovery and everyone was concerned and elated to see his progress. You could see even the men tear up when they would witness his success and if they had not seen him for a couple of weeks they would just stand there and act amazed. It was hard for everyone to hold back the tears when watching him. This man could not walk on the ground, but he could walk in the water. I found myself smiling all the time; it was such a positive environment that we got so much from, and you could see others were so affected by the entire experience of witnessing him with his progression and attitude.

We did our best to go every day after lunch when it was not so busy; we'd take our time afterward to get him bathed and dressed. One of the issues we had was the ability for me to shower him and change his clothes. The "Family" room, or handicapped room, was ideal. Before every workout, I could change him into a bathing suit at the gym, shower him before he went in, and take care of his needs, Then, after, I could shower him again, change his clothes, and get him all bundled to go outside. This is the best way to clean your patient if you ever find yourself in a similar situation.

As the months went by and I had to put more time into working, we were able to find friends who would take him once a week and give me a break. After a year went by, his entire aquatics schedule was booked with friends, and he could take care of scheduling them himself. Gary had Mondays and Wednesdays, Tom had Tuesdays and Thursdays and George had Fridays. He would invite them to lunch afterward, and they'd sit around and just talk; it was so good for him.

Bill walking in water

THERAPY

When he got home from California, we worked on scheduling physical and occupational therapy. I knew before he went to Los Angeles that he was entitled to these services and found out even more once he got home. Cheryl, who had been our great therapist at Genesis, also worked part-time as a contract home-care therapist. We found out that once we completed our at-home therapy from this company, we would end up going to their building a half hour away twice a week.

In the beginning, we had Trish and Judith come to the house from ProCare and they worked on the continuation of his training; they'd keep asking me, "What more do you want me to train him on?" They would walk him with his walker, do core exercises, and do steps. In the beginning, he would get so exhausted climbing stairs that after two or three steps, they'd let him sit down. When Trish asked me "Now what do you want him to do?" I would just say keep climbing stairs, some day he might have to climb on his own. Also, keep working on his falls. When he falls, he needs to find a way to get up on his own. Judith had him working on everything occupational like picking up money with the left hand, folding clothes, standing at the sink, and doing dishes; all kinds of movements that he no longer could do because he was paralyzed.

THE 35 RULE

No one ever actually said there was a "35 Rule" and I never saw it in writing, but I had heard of it somewhere, I just never could remember. Once I understood what the 35 Rule was, I could fully understand what it was to a person who was paralyzed and retraining their brain to think on its own without the constant reminder of what to do. Rewiring the brain and having the neuro-receptors redirect themselves can be tricky; you need to outsmart the brain and get it to think differently.

Here is the best thing to remember: when you are starting your walk, it is a little rough at the beginning of your routine. You need to tell yourself to lift, lock, lift, lock. On the 35th time, your brain kicks in and does it automatically and you are retraining your brain. Tomorrow you will do this all over again, and on the 35th time, it will kick in again. Each day you do this, it gets a little easier. If by chance you skip a few days, you will more than likely have to start like it was similar to day one; however, everyone is different. We did find that if you did these two or three times a day, your brain was retraining even faster. He no longer has to count steps or say "Lift, Lock."

We also saw this with occupational therapy. While training him to pick up marbles and put them in a bottle, after the 35th time he was a natural. The key to anything when you are training your brain is repetition. The more you do this and the more times a day you do this and do it for over a month, your ability to grab a marble with your paralyzed fingers and get them into the bottle gets so much easier. We made this a game with the little grandkids, they were training Grandpa and they would pick up his "lost marbles" saying "Grandpa, you are losing your marbles." Find the humor and get the whole family into the laugh, it does help to unite the family into helping in the care.

This 35 Rule is good in so many other ways; A basketball player does a repetitive motion on the 3-point shot 35 times every day for days from the same location, more chances than not will get it every time. This is the same with foul shooting or even a jump shot. Repetitive motion 35 times seems to be the number used to get your body to recognize its natural moves.

The stairs can also fall under the 35 Rule. There are generally 13 stairs up and 13 stairs down. He would climb up going forward and climb down going backward. This took a while, and it was not a quick learn but he can do it if he holds on to the rails on both sides. He did it so much that he now makes it to the 4th floor climbing up the entire flight without me holding my breath and hovering over him. It is really important that we have handrails on both sides of the stairs and that he is extra cautious and goes slow. Now when we go to our friend's house for dinner or parties, we can get him in and out without too much trouble. Our lives opened up so much more after he could climb a few stairs.

Socializing

Bill was not very social after the stroke. His friends would come to visit him, and he would talk with them for about 5 minutes and then fall asleep, or he would just look straight ahead waiting for you to do all of the talking. I had made him aware of what he was doing and how he came across. Strokes really do fuzz up your brain and I really do not think he was aware of how he came across until I said something. In all fairness to the patient, if you can tell them in a nice way and do it privately, they really do appreciate your constructive criticism. They too want to come across as a healing person and not a limp victim.

I felt bad for him, but I knew that if I did not keep pushing him, he was not going to advance. I know I exhausted him with his exercising and making sure he was keeping up with his training, but I also knew sleep was important too. Stroke victims need their sleep more than ever in order to recover. I did try to keep his social time to when I knew he would be rested. If he had been to the pool, I knew he needed a 2-hour nap. As much as I wanted my social life back, I knew he wanted it as well and he was feeling guilty that he was keeping me from getting out with my friends.

I made a long list of people who are his friends, wrote their phone numbers, and entered all of this into his phone. I was trying to get him to take control of his life and not rely on me to make his schedule and ask people to take him places. It took time for him to actually ask for rides or pool partners, but once he got the hang of it, he was more comfortable.

One of his great friends introduced him to the ROMEO group. It is an acronym for Retired Old Men Eating Out. To this day, they meet every Monday morning and eat breakfast together. He really needs this time with the guys and to shoot the bull with old-retired men. His buddy, Leo, would pick him up and take him and watch over him. It became a great friendship with other old-retired men who had once had a career and are looking to fill their time.

He also has kept up with his other group, "Men's Night Out." Once a month they would all meet at one of the guys' houses and they'd all bring part of the meal and every month they'd rotate. After eating, they play games, drink, laugh, and do whatever else old men do when they get together. We wives in turn go out to a nice restaurant and enjoy our time alone. It works for both of us. Everyone is so good about getting Bill into their houses and getting him comfortable. He likes feeling like he is still one of the guys.

We try to go out to eat at least once every two weeks. In the beginning, I shied away from it; it got easier as I saw how our friends were so helpful. I also found that people in restaurants who see someone in a wheelchair are more than willing to help. I will admit, we go early and not when the lines are out the door. Yes, there are many issues with a paralyzed body, your lips are also paralyzed; you do not know when the food is flowing down your chin. I carefully take my napkin and look at him and wipe my own lips and chin; allowing him the suttel hint to wipe it up.

I have encouraged Bill to do as much socializing as he is willing to do. I really pushed him to meet new people and have a life outside of the stroke. I had seen how the guys at Next Steps Fitness in California would also go to lunch or eat in the lunchroom. They were used to their paralysis and found it easier to get around as they'd had a lot of time to adapt. They were good at helping Bill to accept his affliction and not hold him back; he had realized his life was going to be OK.

Times to Find Laughter

It is hard to find laughter when you are depressed and have no idea where you are going to be in a month or two. However, you have to remain lighthearted, smile, and laugh; people will flock to you to be a part of your happiness, but not to your anger or sadness. Have some funny stories to tell and make sure your partner finds it funny too, or else it will backfire on you.

I used to take Bill to the pool daily for his exercise and walk in the water. I would wheel him in and two of the guys would help me get him into the handicapped pool chair that would drop him into the water. This one time, two young guys were lifting him up and I was adjusting the straps. Bill started flailing with his left paralyzed hand getting it caught in my bathing suit strap. As he was trying to get his fingers to release, he pulled down my suit, exposing one of the "Girls" to all who were there. I do not know who was more embarrassed.

One morning we were lying in bed still sleeping, I slept on his left paralyzed side, and I reached over to gently rub his arm, chest, face, and shoulder. He did not feel a thing, so I was not concerned about waking him. He cracked his eye open, looked over, closed his eye again, and brought his right hand up to touch mine, all while smiling with appreciation for the affection. As I got out of bed, he noticed he was still rubbing a hand, but it was not mine; it was his left paralyzed hand. I swear, he laughed for months telling that story and his friends loved the story as he told it over and over again.

We found playing games was great entertainment for him. He loves games that do not require two hands and yet he has to use his brain. Dominoes, Scrabble, and cards are just a few. He also has great fun watching everyone play "What's Up", offering his answers and suggestions along the way.

He has also found so much joy in playing with the grandkids. During the COVID times, he has been doing schoolwork with our youngest 8-year-old grandson and helping the 17-year-old grandson with his AP classes and online schooling. With our little 5-year-old granddaughter, he colors and plays dolls, horses, dinosaurs, you name it, even dominoes. He loves to do this as it brings so much laughter to his heart and the kids get to see Grandpa in a fun way.

Little Squirt Luna squirting Grandpa

Bill & me at Halloween

Handicapped Areas

I got Bill's application and placard when he had his hip and knee surgeries but I asked the doctor to have another one filled out so it was for forever and he could have it extended. You can go online to download the form, have the doctor sign it, and mail it in. The process is not hard, it is just time-consuming and daunting. You cannot just go in and get one, it takes at least 2 weeks. Do this right away; get the signature so when they finally do come home you have the placard.

I have always been disappointed with people who park in handicapped parking spots who are not walking with a cane, in a wheelchair, or using a walker. I know there are many who would disagree with my comments, but there are so many times that these spots are taken, and we cannot park close enough or have enough space to get him out of the car.

I have my placard in the window, and you can see the wheelchair and walker in the backseat, so you would think others would be sympathetic and not fight you for the spot. Sometimes if I am not in a hurry, I will stay behind the row of handicapped parked cars and wait for the drivers to come and leave. I would say more than 50% of the time they are not handicapped or appear to be using someone else's card.

The one time I went to the DMV and did this same thing waiting for a spot to open, I watched a young girl come running out and jump in her car that was parked in the zone, and the police officer stood right there and said nothing. I even asked the police officer if he saw that, and he just nonchalantly said "No." I really do not think others see or understand your predicament until they themselves are in it. I cannot always leave him in the car, it gets too hot or too cold and it would require me to leave the car running to keep him comfortable.

I wish there was a way to get each state to recognize the misuse of these placards and introduce legislation that would penalize those who misuse the card. The only idea I had that I thought would be helpful was to put on the front of the placard, "Female 1940," or "Male 1945". This would at least alleviate those who want to use Grandma's placard to get a better parking spot.

I would also like to see different colors on the placards or stickers. A Heart for those who cannot walk far for fear of a heart attack, a wheelchair for those afflicted in their legs or back, and something for "too old" like a man bent over with a cane.

I would also like to see signage on the Family Rooms that are equipped with a larger toilet area for those in a wheelchair. If the signage read: "For wheelchairs and young families only" and NOT those who need to change their clothes or use the room as their private restroom.

The Veterans Benefits

I wanted to touch on the veterans' benefits shortly after the Handicapped chapter because this story goes hand in hand with the topic.

When Bill was in LA, we went to the Los Angeles VA Hospital. It is a huge old complex with very nice people and an older facility that is still held together and maintained, but not updated. He was in his wheelchair and I struggled to get him in and out of the car and then into the building. It was not easy.

When he had to use the restroom, I asked if they had a Family Restroom that I could take him into. Here is this huge facility and not one Family Restroom! Now how do I get him into a stall at the VA? How do I lift him up, turn him around and onto the toilet, let him sit there for a while, and come back to clean him up? They actually struggled with this and ended up closing off the doctor's lounge, getting him into a different chair that would fit into the opened handicapped stall, and I sat outside in a chair until he called for me. This should never happen to anyone, let alone a Veteran.

The VA staff in both Providence and LA are fantastic, they both are run with adequate efficiency and welcoming staff. Providence has made the upgrades to the handicapped bathrooms. In both LA and Providence, there are very old VA buildings that have not been renovated and are never going to be perfect. The new construction has been great, but they need to do a lot more to get up to the standards of even basic hospitals. However, if you find out how to use the VA and talk to the correct people, you will find the most dedicated people who are overworked and very pleasant. I truly feel if you can understand those issues, you can appreciate everything they do for the veterans; most of the staff are veterans themselves.

I have kept huge files for all of his care and each type of care is kept in a separate file. The VA file was so big that I had to put the entire file in a canvas bag so I could easily pick it up and run with it or access it without a massive search. I have also scanned every document so I can find it on my computer. I found that the VA has so little time to deal with each person, it is best to be prepared and efficient. I am going to go into stages of how things are accomplished; hopefully it will help others.

- Have your veteran's complete personal file with discharge papers, entry papers, and every bit of data you can find on them. I have these specific numbers on a card for fast access.

- It is good to get yourself registered at the VA in your area in advance, without having to wait for something to happen to you. You will get a VA card and number for your wallet.

- If you were in a Foreign War or conflict area, the VA can pull up absolutely everything about you, where you were docked/assigned, what you were exposed to, reports of any injuries and treatments, if you could have been exposed to a hearing loss or lung exposure, you name it, their records are extremely complete.

- In your paperwork you are going to need all of your personal doctors, their numbers, and your case file, and from here on out, every time you have an appointment with any of these doctors you will send them the paperwork for their files too.

- Have them give you a % disability rating; they then give you a service-connected evaluation level. You may possibly get a monthly check award (not retroactive) for your military service affliction or disability. A couple hundred each month does not hurt.

- In many cases, but not all, the VA may outfit your house or contribute to the process of building out your home to help you adapt to your disability. It is a grant, so it does require you to fill out lots of papers and it does go through a review process.

- When Bill had his stroke, I asked them for an advocate, they assigned a great guy who came to the nursing home and sat with us, filled out paperwork, and helped us to get to the proper areas of the veteran's services that would be helpful to us. Jack Ryan was ours and he was a Godsend. If I had a question, I called Jack; he worked in the same office as one of our Senators, so he had the connections to see things through if need be.

- I gave his Occupational Therapist at the nursing home the phone number of the person at the VA where we could order handicapped everything! When the truck pulled up, I was overwhelmed with brand new equipment, and it was the best, not the shoddy equipment Medicare was allowing us that I was actually billed for.

- I also obtained a VA Social Worker that I could call anytime, and they would get back to me with who to contact or what to do.

- We were assigned an Occupational Therapist. If Bill was bedridden, he might qualify to have someone come to our house.

- I did not know if Bill was going to ever be able to come home and live, so I also filled out all of the forms for the Veterans' Nursing Home. Fortunately, we never had to use it, but there was a long waiting list, and it was going to absorb all of his Social Security checks. I had to be prepared in advance, and you need to be aware of what there is to worry about.
- He was also eligible to have the VA come to our house, pick him up, and take him to the VA. We never had to use this service, but knowing it was available was helpful.
- He was assigned a Personal Physician. She has been his doctor there since he had heart issues and knee and hip surgery.

I did not know where in the book I should say what I have been saying to myself for so long, but this seems to be the best place to say something from my heart. When I see how so many Veterans have come home and how their afflictions happened so early in life, I have to thank God this was not our case. I would also say that if these families can take care of their injured Veterans, I can too. I know I do not have it half as hard as they do, and I lived my life.

The VA is a great service, and it is to your benefit to know as much as you can in advance, so you do not go into a helter-skelter tirade. See the end for various documents, forms, and pages from the VA for help.

Choosing Your Doctors and Care

Most of the time you are assigned a doctor for your specialized care at the public hospital. We were fortunate in most of our cases to get the best doctors for Bill, and they worked with us and appreciated our desire to not accept the outcome. I personally was not going to work with any doctor who was negative and not willing to help us find a way to have Bill walk. I know so many were confident he would never walk again, but the word "NEVER" was not in our vocabulary. I dismissed those who could not give us hope and went with those who would support us in a positive way.

Fortunately, his Neurologist, Dr. Shawna Cutting, could see we were not your ordinary couple who took "never" as a final word; all she heard from us was that we would find a way. She passed on various ideas, looked up clinical trials for Bill, and wished him well to go to California for locomotor training at Next Steps Fitness. Her encouragement and letter writing to get him into various programs were helpful for us to know that she thought there was hope.

She explained that so many go through a stroke and give up. There is so much pain to work through and most of the time you are so defeated. It happens and I can see where this would happen to any stroke victim, especially those who have had a hemorrhage. If you do not have a partner who is willing to be your advocate and push harder than you are willing to push yourself, you will likely see yourself fail. Find that advocate and find a way to make them happy while they are trying to help you. Don't be the downer, say the positive words and be ever so grateful.

I have spoken to so many people who are caring for their spouse who have had a stroke. Most of these people are afraid to motivate their patients hard and make them push themselves. If Bill had not allowed me to be firm and set things up and force him to do things, I do not think he would have done most of what was offered. He would hate it when I would be persistent (aka nag), but I would just follow up with, "It's up to you if you want to improve."

I have Bill keep his own calendar of doctor, aquatic, and therapy appointments. I know he still has the ability to use his phone, so he can use the tools on his phone too. He sends me reminders of every appointment so I can have them on my schedule too. If I cannot take him, he can phone a friend and ask for help. He gets reminders, so he is not forgetting his scheduled events. He really does well with this, and it has worked out perfectly.

Bill could get to the beach

117

Making Everything Work

No one has really had to adjust anything to accommodate him, we have found ways to adapt ourselves. I do my best to not do everything for him and push him to do it himself, even if it takes 10 times longer. He has to find a way, even if he fails.

I have been traveling quite a bit and I leave him at home. I have gone for up to a week, and he managed well. I do have it so he has someone calling him in the morning, taking him somewhere in the afternoon, and again calling him at night. Our daughters also keep calling him and making sure he is doing OK. I have meals all cooked; all he has to do is heat them up in the microwave. I also found there were those who would bring him meals as well, so he never starved. I also called him at least 3 times a day, and he would text me with any needs.

He also has lots of chores around the house. Once he was able to stand and do exercises at the kitchen counter, he took over rinsing the dishes and putting them in the dishwasher, wiping the counters, and putting things away. His walker has a seat, so he loads up the seat, takes the plates and silverware to the table, and sets it up for dinner. He also folds clothing and sorts them so I can put them away. He has his chores, and he makes his own list. When he is in Los Angeles, he waters the plants outside and picks off the dead leaves. Once he was home, he would buy the same book my grandson, and with the use of Facetime read together and help with homework. He earns his keep, and he feels good that he can contribute.

The Latest Technology

It goes without saying, when you are in Bill's situation you are always looking for the latest technology to come along that is not going to break the bank and is going to improve your life. We are in constant search for the latest and greatest, either in a clinical trial or something that might be worth trying.

Recently, my daughter met a fitness coach who was offering a technology for athletes to use to help recover from severe strains and muscle injuries and improve muscle performance. This technology has been used and fully accepted in the European, Asian, and African countries for years and was recently approved in the US by the FDA in Jan. 2019 for rebounding human muscles. She was using it on pro athletes, stunt workers, and runners; she had asked my daughter if she'd be interested. All my daughter could think about was her father; can this improve his paralyzed side and help him?

This Swiss company, WINTECARE™, has what they call "T-Plus Technology"® that uses a tool called a "tekar"® that works at getting immediate results in three applied areas of physical therapy: rehabilitation, performance, and physical conditioning. The machine is used for injuries, post-surgery care, inflammation, or straightforward muscular and osteoarticular pain. My husband wanted to see what it would do for his paralysis.

When Bill walks, he feels like he is dragging a 50-pound leg around. It is extremely exhausting for him, but he has adapted to this movement. Even in the water, when he is walking, he has to lift and move this heavy leg; the same thing also happens with his arm, it is so heavy to move around. After two treatments Bill has been able to walk and lift his leg as if it weighed 10 lbs., and not 50. He can now move his arm and rotate the shoulder like the arm is a windmill.

His coach then moved him to the water where he was to "run" not walk. He was amazed at how fast he could go, and he was lifting his leg so much easier. When he falls in the water, usually someone has to pick him up and hold him until he is steady enough to resume. When he fell this time, his coach said to him, "Get up, you can do it, get yourself over to the side." Lo and behold, he swam over to the side! He could never do that before; he would have been flailing in the water until someone could recover him.

The next day, he went to the LA Fitness gym to use the machines. He sat on the thigh lift machine and lifted the minimum weight. It was a sight he and his coach never would have expected if they had not witnessed it themselves. He has since worked in more repetitions and continues to look for more improvement.

We have no idea where this is going to take him or what he is going to be able to do next month, but when you go from laying in a bed being told, "This is it", to walking and lifting a weight with your paralyzed leg, you know there is hope.

Note: Since I wrote this book, I helped my daughter to buy this machine and learn how to use it. She is now treating several people a day, including her father when he comes to visit. It has taken over her physical training business and consumes much of her time treating athletes and stunt people to recover from their injuries in a fraction of the time. She even uses it on her 32 Y/O horse who walks like an old man. He now canters through the field saying "Look at me ladies! I am a hot stud!"

Do not be afraid of new technology, what have you got to lose?

Life and Love

It is never easy to go through any kind of stroke or devastating affliction, but it happens. It happens to more people than we as individuals recognize. It usually causes the patient and caretakers to go into their own world to deal with the results. Until it happens to you, I do not think there are many who can appreciate how hard it really is for everyone involved.

In the US alone, strokes kill over 140,000 people a year and for those who survive, it is the leading cause of serious long-term disability. Almost 800,000 people have a stroke each year; 87% of all strokes are ischemic, in which the blood flow to the brain is blocked, leaving about 10% of the strokes to hemorrhagic (bleeding) in various parts of the brain. You do not hear too much about this category, simply because they usually do not live and they simply say in the autopsy "died of natural causes," or had a stroke, but they do not determine what type of stroke. Those who live are often the ones you see in the nursing home. But that does not mean that has to be your outcome, everything is determined by your and your loved ones determination to choose to live.

It is not easy to sort everything out or try and make sense of everything when you go through something so debilitating, but you need to reach out and not isolate yourself and give up. Let your church friends help out, let people pray for you, let people help you, but do not isolate yourselves and check out.

Finances can be a big part of your decision on what to do, but when you give up and don't pursue every avenue, call in the troops, and accept everyone's gracious offers, you will slow the process and may not win the challenge. If you are on Medicare and have to pay for your own care, look for alternatives and do not let money be what causes you to hold back on moving forward.

Love is a critical part of the entire healing process. You don't have to be gushy with love, but you need to show that you care, and you are there for your partner; you also need to let them know you are not going to leave them and place them in the nursing home forever. I kept on saying to myself, "How would I want to be treated?" and that is how I treated Bill. I cannot say I did everything right or by the textbook, but I did what I did the way I would have wanted it done for me.

Living Life with Normalcy

I wanted so hard to live our lives like we had before; this meant we had to not look at his handicap as something that was holding us back. I had my business travel and would leave him by himself when I had overnights, and I would call in to say "Hi" but not check in to see if he was ok or eating the prepared food. I tried to treat him normally and not like a "mom" checking in on her boy at home. He really did his best to keep the place neat and clean, without damaging anything.

However, he wanted a bottle of red wine once while I was gone. Yes, he did. Yes, he went to great lengths to go to the wine rack (not easy) and get a bottle, carry it to the kitchen with his walker, and then get the cork extractor. When I got home that night all I could see was red "blood" all over the kitchen floor and white cabinets, his walker stranded in the middle of the kitchen floor, and the marks where he had dragged himself into the living room. He yells out "Welcome Home!" and I ask, "Are you OK?" "Only my pride was hurt, and no, I did not drink any wine." Needless to say, he will never drink wine while I am gone. You do your best to not dictate or direct, but to laugh at the life stories you've created to share with others.

We decided to take 3 weeks and go to Mexico. Another couple

would meet us down there the same day and another couple from his high school swimming days were living there for a longer period of time. Both couples shared in the care and helped me get him around without hovering over him. He ran in the pool with his friend for hours at a time getting in his workouts, chatting the entire time. What was the best was the last two days when his friend got him to swim up to 10 strokes. That was a huge achievement. Bill loved having friends to eat with like normal, sit around and have endless chats, and act normal again. Even though he got around with his scooter and walker, he still did it on his own and I did not have to watch over him. Trips like this were good for me too. I needed a vacation just as much as he did, and I was allowed to not worry about anything.

COVID

After our return from our annual vacation to Puerto Vallarta in early 2020, I returned to our daughter's in California. But the day before we left, I tripped and fell flat on my chest. I was in so much pain, but I did not want to call attention to me. I was trying to help my daughter with her torn screen door and took the knife right into the meaty area of my palm.

Bill called Gabi to come home ASAP and told her I was bleeding out. It was pouring out of my hand so fast, I believe I had knicked an artery. Did I say I also had a flight in two hours? She drove me to CVS on the way to the airport and bought a bag of bandages and tape, and she wrapped it tight to stop the bleeding so I could fly without alarming people.

I returned to Rhode Island. Within the first day of my return, I had to go and have my newly gashed deep cut in the palm of my left hand bandaged and stitched again, then get an x-ray of my 3 broken ribs from my fall. The next morning went to the hospital to get my scalp shaved and have another minor brain surgery on my ever-present meningioma. It was good that I had the time to recover alone and did not have to take care of anyone, as I looked like I'd been in a horrible accident.

This was at the start of COVID. Coming back from Mexico we all chose on our own to take precautions and wear a facemask and I wore one when I went to the hospital. The staff were all concerned I had a cold, and I let them know I was wearing this so I would not get COVID. I was probably ahead of the new game.

COVID restrictions then started to come out and we were all in hibernation role. That was OK since the last thing I wanted to do was go out in public with a shaved head.

Bill stayed in California until May and then returned on his own to the East Coast where he remained sequestered in our house but with very few people to see. His friends were not going to be able to take him for walks or to the gym and he was limited to who he could see. Walking was limited only because he lost his motivation, and I personally did not enjoy pushing him.

I have been able to "encourage" him to walk with a cane around the house. He was not going outside in the cold weather and preferred to sit in his recliner reading his phone. When he pushed back on me, I reminded him how his 8-year-old grandson could not wait to see him walk with a cane and not a walker. Bingo! The cane is now used at least 10% of the time and he takes walks outside with his walker and a cane (and me). Yes, he has fallen and yes, he does bruise, but it all heals, and he moves on. If it looks bad, I take him to the doctor's but to date, that has only happened twice in 3 years.

I hear that often times the stroke person feels that it is OK to lash out at those who are family, even when they are doing their best to be kind and caring. They want to do what they want to do, not what you suggest. I get that, but I do not understand why they feel they have the ability to say whatever they want and get away with it. I often say to my husband, "Would you say the same thing to our daughters or to your friends?" It is painful and challenging as the caretaker to be the one that is abused; but get used to it, you are the only one they know they can do things to and get away with it. Sometimes you just need to take a break and have a little separation for a few days, then when you come back, they see you as an angel and not a devil in disguise.

Friendship real in Puerto Vallarta, Mexico

Mike and Bill

Nothing but two friends from high-school, on the same swim team and born on the same day in the same state and still keeping the friendship real.

131

Bill and our then 17 YO

When you cannot stand you do not have the ability to measure up to your just turned 15 Y/O grandson who has now towered over the ol' man he has always looked up to. And the little angel laughs with joy knowing she is the next one to grow tall like grandpa

Yes, he pushes her around on the walker and she loves it as much as he does.

Nothing like a surprise little squirt going to water world
with Grandpa, they laughed forever!

Conclusion

I know there is so much more I can say and write about, but at some point, I have had to say, "I have reached my plateau." I know this is not about me, but in reality, as the caretaker, it is about me too. Yes, he is the patient, but I have been affected by all of this too. I am tired of pushing, hearing back talk, and not feeling whole either. It is much like Bill: he does not feel whole, but he is happy to have what he has, and he is thankful for his accomplishment through all of these past 3 years. He hates to be pushed and he is tired of only seeing me and my daughter and grandkids that come frequently to visit, but life is not the same and sequestering has taken its toll on us all. COVID had an adverse effect on many people; he was not alone.

I still like to repeat the ol' "CANI" phrase: Constant and Never-ending Improvement. If you are not going for the CANI, you will plateau and you will only stay with what you have accomplished. The Rule of 35, the tools purchased for him, all of the hand games, leg games, exercise machines, exercise instructions, and things he has been taught have been donated or are no longer necessary. COVID and sequestering have put a damper on everything, but at some point, I hope he will do his best to push harder and do something more than sit around and read from his phone. We will eventually get back into the pool, it will get warmer, and he will get outside more to walk and visit with neighbors. It is OK to plateau, you just have to recognize when you hit the plateau you need to change directions.

Post Conclusion

It has now been 7-1/2 years since the stroke. I had written this during COVID and had sent it out to many publishers trying to get this published. Unfortunately, I was not one of the successful authors who wrote a gripping story that challenged you or caused you to cry. I only wanted to share our story and show others to never give up. Bill has not changed much but he has not digressed. Yes, he still falls a couple of times a week and he still struggles with everyday challenges. His immediate family still challenge him to push himself harder and not sit around looking at his phone. However, he is happy, and he is still loving life, all because no one gave up on him.

Printed in the United States
by Baker & Taylor Publisher Services